HAZLETON PUBLISHING

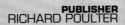
PUBLISHER
RICHARD POULTER

EDITOR
SIMON ARRON

WRITTEN BY
PIERO ALBERGHI & SIMON ARRON

ART EDITOR
RYAN BAPTISTE

RESULTS & DATA
DAVID HAYHOE

PRODUCTION MANAGER
STEVEN PALMER

PUBLISHING DEVELOPMENT MANAGER
SIMON SANDERSON

SALES PROMOTION
ANNALISA ZANELLA

MARKETING & NEW MEDIA MANAGER
NICK POULTER

PHOTOGRAPHY
LAT PHOTOGRAPHIC

CAR GRAPHICS
RUSSELL LEWIS

ALL RESULTS AND DATA
© FIA 2000

GRAND PRIX YEAR

is published by
Hazleton Publishing Ltd.,
3 Richmond Hill,
Richmond, Surrey
TW10 6RE, England.

**Colour reproduction by
HBS Design Associates Ltd, Newbury.**

**Printed in England by
HBS Design Associates Ltd, Newbury.**

ISBN: 1-874557 89 6

FEATURES

www.hazletonpublishing.com

DISTRIBUTORS

UNITED KINGDOM
Haynes Publishing
Sparkford
Nr Yeovil
Somerset
BA22 7JJ
Tel: 01963 440635
Fax: 01963 440001

NORTH AMERICA
Motorbooks
International
PO Box 1
729 Prospect Ave.
Osceola
Wisconsin 54020, USA
Tel: (1) 715 294 3345
Fax: (1) 715 294 4448

REST OF THE WORLD
Menoshire Ltd
Unit 13
Wadsworth Road
Perivale
Middlesex UB6 7LQ
Tel: 020 8566 7344
Fax: 020 8991 2439

2000 FIA FORMULA ONE WORLD CHAMPIONSHIP

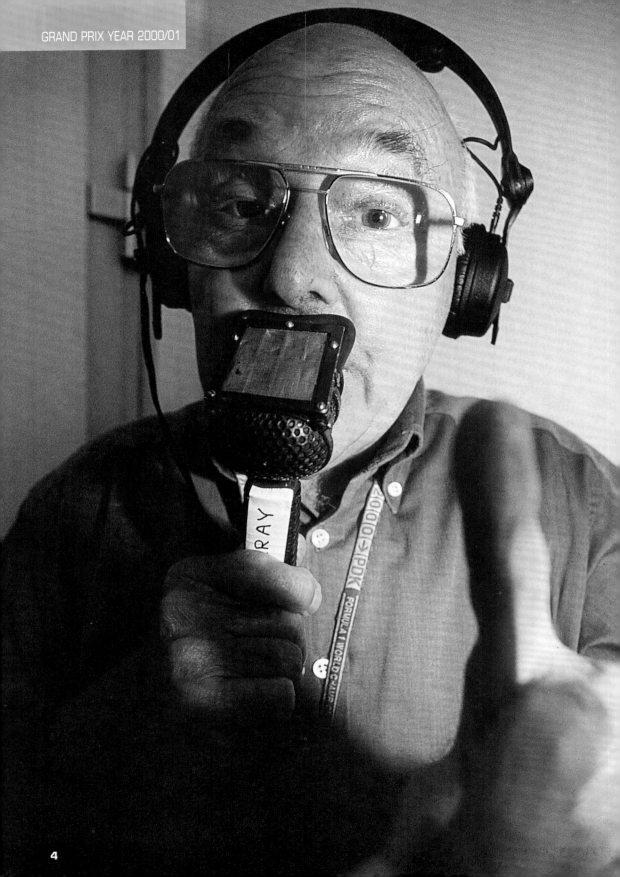

FOREWORD
BY MURRAY WALKER

IT FEELS LIKE ONLY YESTERDAY THAT I WAS AT MONZA, WATCHING JODY
Scheckter and Gilles Villeneuve finish first and second to secure the
1979 world title for Ferrari – the third time in a decade that the men
from Maranello had clinched the championship for drivers.

I don't suppose any of us thought it would be another 21 years
before they might repeat the trick. Just imagine, that was before
Alain Prost or Nigel Mansell had made their first grand prix start –
and Michael Schumacher was only 10!

Finally, this year, Schuey brought that long drought to an
end – and few will begrudge him that. Whatever the politics and
machinations that have marked recent grand prix seasons, the
German's greatness has never been in question and he has added a
spark to many races that might otherwise have been consigned to
history's forgettable file.

Truth be told, however, Mika Hakkinen would have been just as
worthy a recipient of the crown. Judged objectively, these two are
very hard to separate and their recent battles have been a compelling
highlight for me and, I suspect, millions of others.

As I write, the dust has barely settled on this season's Malaysian
finale, but as I prepare for a couple of months of [relative] calm my
thoughts are already on 2001.

Can Ferrari hang on? Will McLaren bounce back? Might Williams'
highly-rated new signing Juan Pablo Montoya beat all of them? And
could Jenson Button force Williams to regret its choice to loan him
out to Benetton and Renault?

There is, as always, so much to look forward to. First, however, it is
my pleasure to welcome readers to Grand Prix Year – which remains
a colourful, comprehensive and irreverent review of the season just
past. I hope you'll enjoy reading it as much as I know I will.

THE CLASS OF 2000

TIME WAS WHEN THE GRAND PRIX PADDOCK WAS AWASH WITH DOG-EARED TEAMS WHO SPENT LESS IN A SEASON ON THEIR CARS AND ENGINES THAN McLAREN DID ON TABLE NAPKINS. BUT NO MORE. THE BERNIE-FRIENDLY WORLD OF MODERN F1 IS FULL OF SUPER-SLICK OPERATORS – AND EVEN IF MINARDI DOES HAVE A PREFERENCE FOR PAPER PLATES, ITS SPAGHETTI SPRINKLED WITH PARMESAN IS STILL ABSOLUTELY DELICIOUS

McLaren MP4-15

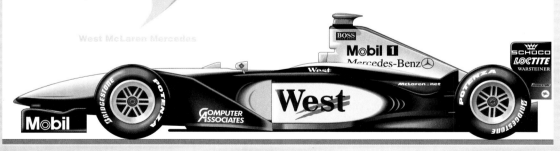

McLAREN-MERCEDES

DRIVERS: MIKA HAKKINEN, FIN [LEFT], DAVID COULTHARD, GB [RIGHT]
TESTER: OLIVIER PANIS, F

Pre-season prospects: Calm. Driver pairing entering fifth year together. Adrian Newey still heading up design team. Colossal budget [though they could get even more if they sold advertising space on Mika Hakkinen's wife, who is on TV almost as often as he is]
2001 LINE-UP: Unchanged

Ferrari F1-2000

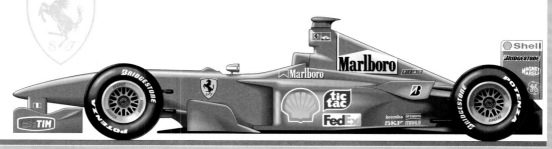

FERRARI

DRIVER: MICHAEL SCHUMACHER, D [LEFT]
SACRIFICIAL LAMB: RUBENS BARRICHELLO, BR [RIGHT]
TESTER: LUCA BADOER, I

Pre-season prospects: Allegedly not chaotic. They'd been paying Schuey 20-odd million quid per season for four years, and all they had to show was a solitary championship title for constructors. Still, it was the only thing they'd won since 1983. Barrichello – effectively number two in a one-car team, despite protestations to the contrary – came in promising to take the fight to Schuey. Plausibility not pictured
2001 LINE-UP: Unchanged

Jordan EJ10

JORDAN- MUGEN HONDA

DRIVERS: HEINZ-HARALD FRENTZEN, D [LEFT], JARNO TRULLI, I [RIGHT]
TESTER, ALBEIT ALMOST INVISIBLE: TOMAS ENGE, CZ

Pre-season prospects: Formidable. Third in the constructors' championship the previous season. Highly-rated Trulli in for the retired Damon Hill. What could possibly go wrong? Bang! Oh...
2001 LINE-UP: Drivers unchanged; works Honda engine deal

Jaguar R1

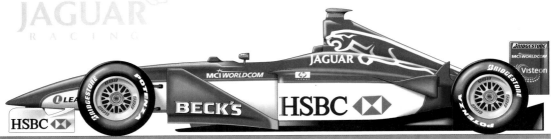

JAGUAR-COSWORTH

DRIVERS: EDDIE IRVINE, GB [LEFT], JOHNNY HERBERT, GB [RIGHT]
TESTERS: LUCIANO BURTI, BR, TOMAS SCHECKTER, ZA,
NARAIN KARTHIKEYAN, IND

Pre-season prospects: Uncertain. Dosh not a problem
following parent company Ford's takeover of former Stewart
GP team. But creating a basis from which to challenge
McLaren and Ferrari requires more than money alone. And
team leader Irvine had consistently been unable to match
Michael Schumacher in four seasons at Ferrari
2001 LINE-UP: Irvine remains, Burti replaces Herbert

Williams FW22

WILLIAMS-BMW

DRIVERS: RALF SCHUMACHER, D [LEFT], JENSON BUTTON, GB [RIGHT]
TESTER: BRUNO JUNQUEIRA, BR

Pre-season prospects: Fantastic or flimsy, depending on
your standpoint. Good news: BMW back in F1. Bad news:
Germans hadn't run an F1 engine since 1987. More good
news: Button looks very promising. More bad news: He's not
old enough to hire from Hertz or Avis and has only raced
cars for two seasons. Still, most eight-year-olds would do a
better job than Alex Zanardi did in 1999
2001 LINE-UP: Schuey Jnr stays, Colombian Champ Car star
Juan Pablo Montoya in for Button

Benetton B200

BENETTON-PLAYLIFE

DRIVERS: GIANCARLO FISICHELLA, I [LEFT], ALEXANDER WURZ, A [RIGHT]
TESTER FOR THE FIRST FIVE MINUTES OF THE SEASON, BEFORE HE WAS
DROPPED: HIDETOSHI MITSUSADA, J
TESTER FOR THE REST OF THE SEASON: JUST ABOUT ANY TEENAGER WHO HAPPENED
TO BE RUNNING WELL IN ANY EUROPEAN F3 SERIES YOU CARED TO MENTION

Pre-season prospects: Moderate. Fisichella's undoubted class likely to be masked by lack of significant technical progress. But back in March we didn't know about the impending Renault takeover. World still waiting for Wurz to produce his first decent drive since Monaco 1998
2001 LINE-UP: Greater input from new owner Renault; Fisichella joined by Williams refugee Jenson Button

Prost AP03

PROST-PEUGEOT

DRIVERS: JEAN ALESI, F [LEFT], NICK HEIDFELD, D [RIGHT]
TESTER: STÉPHANE SARRAZIN, F

Pre-season prospects: Ropey. Final year with engine partner Peugeot, so quantum leaps not likely even before relations became more strained than a dish of Heinz baby food. F1's most experienced campaigner Alesi still fast; F3000 champ Heidfeld rich in potential, but could have done without the car breaking every time he tried to test it
LIKELY 2001 LINE-UP: Alesi nowhere else to go, Pedro Diniz daft enough to want to join him; customer Ferrari engines

Sauber C19

SAUBER-PETRONAS

DRIVERS: MIKA SALO, FIN [LEFT], PEDRO DINIZ, BR [RIGHT]
TESTER: ENRIQUE BERNOLDI, BR

Pre-season prospects: Are you an unambitious midfield plodder? Here's the team for you. Swiss mob always build a capable car, which benefits from rebranded Ferrari engine. Never the worst – but never likely to challenge for much more than fifth place on a good day, either
2001 LINE-UP: Nick Heidfeld confirmed, several others squabbling over second seat at time of going to press

Arrows A21

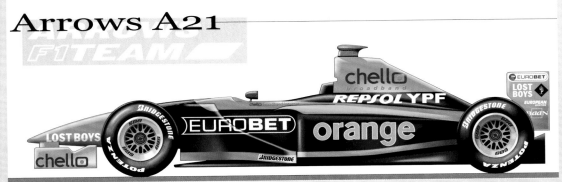

ARROWS-SUPERTEC

DRIVERS: PEDRO DE LA ROSA, E [LEFT], JOS VERSTAPPEN, NL [RIGHT]
TESTER, EXCEPT THE DEAL FELL THROUGH BEFORE HE PROPERLY GOT HIS BUM IN THE CAR: MARK WEBBER, AUS

Pre-season prospects: Better than for many a year. Sensible drivers. Sensible budget. Sensible engine after a couple of seasons struggling along with its own underfinanced V10
PROBABLE 2001 LINE-UP: drivers unchanged; old Peugeot engine – rebadged as AMT – replaces Supertec

Minardi M02

MINARDI-COSWORTH

DRIVER: MARC GENÉ, E [LEFT]
BLOKE PAYING A FORTUNE FOR THE PRIVILEGE OF TOOLING AROUND AT THE BACK: GASTON MAZZACANE, ARG [RIGHT]
TESTERS: FERNANDO ALONSO, E, GIORGIO VINELLA, I

Pre-season prospects: Same as they ever were. Probably the best chassis in Minardi's history. Sod all use, however, if your engine is a couple of evolutionary steps behind the one Ford put in the Model T

2001 LINE-UP: fluid at the time of writing , but Mazzacane probably has enough dosh for them not to kick him out

BAR 002

BAR-HONDA

DRIVERS: JACQUES VILLENEUVE, CDN [LEFT], RICARDO ZONTA, BR [RIGHT]
TESTERS: DARREN MANNING, GB, PATRICK LEMARIÉ, F

Pre-season prospects: Positive. Stable driver line-up. Works Honda V10 cause for genuine optimism after calamity-strewn debut season in 1999. Team less likely to suffer violent migraines after scrapping of 1999's dual livery eyesore
2001 LINE-UP: Villeneuve decided to quit in favour of the Renault-owned Benetton team, then changed his mind; Olivier Panis usurps Zonta

[ARGUABLY] VITAL STATISTICS

YOUR AT-A-GLANCE GUIDE TO SETTLE BAR DISPUTES. HAS MICHAEL SCHUMACHER DONE ENOUGH TO DESERVE A L'ORÉAL ENDORSEMENT CONTRACT, WHICH PUB WERE YOU IN WHEN JENSON BUTTON WAS BORN – AND WHY ARE FERRARI AND McLAREN THE ONLY TEAMS NOT TO HAVE GIVEN AT LEAST ONE CURRENT DRIVER HIS GP DEBUT?

DRIVER	BORN	FIRST GP START
Jean Alesi	Jun 11 1964	France 1989, Tyrrell
Rubens Barrichello	May 23 1972	South Africa 1993, Jordan
Luciano Burti	Mar 5 1973	Austria 2000, Jaguar
Jenson Button	Jan 18 1980	Australia 2000, Williams
David Coulthard	Mar 27 1971	Spain 1994, Williams
Pedro de la Rosa	Feb 24 1971	Australia 1999, Arrows
Pedro Diniz	May 22 1970	Brazil 1995, Forti
Giancarlo Fisichella	Jan 14 1973	Australia 1996, Minardi
Heinz-Harald Frentzen	May 18 1967	Brazil 1994, Sauber
Marc Gené	Mar 29 1974	Australia 1999, Minardi
Mika Hakkinen	Sep 28 1968	America 1991, Lotus
Nick Heidfeld	May 10 1977	Australia 2000, Prost
Johnny Herbert	Jun 25 1964	Brazil 1989, Benetton
Eddie Irvine	Nov 10 1965	Japan 1993, Jordan
Gaston Mazzacane	May 8 1975	Australia 2000, Minardi
Mika Salo	Nov 30 1966	Japan 1994, Lotus
Michael Schumacher	Jan 3 1969	Belgium 1991, Jordan
Ralf Schumacher	Jun 20 1975	Australia 1997, Jordan
Jarno Trulli	Jul 13 1974	Australia 1997, Minardi
Jos Verstappen	Mar 4 1972	Brazil 1994, Benetton
Jacques Villeneuve	Apr 9 1971	Australia 1996, Williams
Alexander Wurz	Feb 15 1974	Canada 1997, Benetton
Ricardo Zonta	Mar 23 1976	Australia 1999, BAR

TOTAL STARTS	WINS	POLE POSITIONS	POINTS SCORED
184	1	2	236
130	1	3	139
1	0	0	0
17	0	0	12
107	9	10	294
33	0	0	3
98	0	0	10
74	0	1	67
114	3	2	153
33	0	0	1
145	18	26	383
16	0	0	0
161	3	0	98
113	4	0	177
17	0	0	0
93	0	0	31
144	44	31	600 [678*]
66	0	0	86
62	0	0	17
74	0	0	16
82	11	13	197
52	0	0	26
29	0	0	2

* deprived of 78 points in 1997 for being a thug

QANTAS AUSTRALIAN GRAND PRIX

FOR THE FIRST TIME
IN FIVE SEASONS AT
FERRARI, SCHUEY GETS
OFF TO A WINNING START
BECAUSE McLAREN PITCHES
UP WITH A CAR THAT'S FAST –
BUT MORE TEMPERAMENTAL
THAN PATRICK VIEIRA

Red spread: he might have been born in a country
with rubbish cuisine, but Michael Schumacher
(left) knew the recipe for success in Australia.
Above, Ferrari congratulates Rubens Barrichello
for finishing on the same lap as his team-mate

ANYONE WHO UNDERSTANDS GRAND PRIX RACING knows that Formula One's head honcho Bernie Ecclestone likes things to be well drilled, perfectly ironed and immaculately presented. Regular, in a word.

Even by his standards, however, there was something spookily regimented about qualifying at the Australian Grand Prix in Melbourne. The top three on the grid were the same as they had been for the last two years. The first five were the same as they were in 1999. And the fastest seven drivers lined up in numerical order.

Race day might have jogged a few memories as well, because the two McLarens sprinted away before succumbing to mechanical mayhem and handing victory to Ferrari. Plus ça change...

Michael Schumacher had no complaints. The German took victory in the opening race of the campaign for the first time since he last won the championship, in 1995. And, something of a novelty since he signed up with the Prancing Horse, his car looked competitive from day one. For his rivals, there could have been few more ominous portents.

"Delighted is probably the wrong word – relief is more like it," the champagne-soaked Schumacher said. "It's the fifth time Ferrari and I have tried to get it right from the start, but when I got into the new car I immediately felt it was going to win. It's reliable and so bloody fast.

"I think we are up with the McLarens," he added, by way of a sideswipe, "because I was not pushing too hard early on when they were in front. I'd say we are there."

HIS CAR LOOKED COMPETITIVE FROM DAY ONE. FOR HIS RIVALS, THERE COULD HAVE BEEN FEW MORE OMINOUS PORTENTS

Peach Melbourne: Schuey cuts through the shadows en route to victory (above). His younger brother picked up some silverware on BMW's successful return to F1 (right). The Jaguars were a) green and b) useless (below)

PAIR WILLIAMS

In Cinderella, Buttons doesn't get to go to the ball. In real life, meanwhile, Button was too busy acting out his own fairy tale.

Back in January, 20-year-old Jenson Button – a former karting ace with two years of car racing under his belt – had been eagerly anticipating the new grand prix season. Little could he have known he would be sitting on the grid when the start flights flicked on and off in Melbourne.

Unless you were cryogenically frozen for the first few months of the year, you'll know the story. Williams dropped the disappointing Alex Zanardi, found there were few logical replacements available and had to extend its search. Tipped off by Prost Grand Prix, for whom Button [left, above, with Williams technical boss Patrick Head] had tested impressively in December, it found a new team-mate for Ralf Schmacher in an unlikely source and sparked a frenzy of newspaper headline puns [Button flies, Button up etc etc] that endured for the season – and left none spare for us to use here.

Few could have predicted the impact Button would make in Melbourne. The Englishman crashed heavily in Saturday practice and had only four laps to prepare for qualifying. Then a fuel pressure problem before the session forced him to switch to the spare car, he qualified 21st and the press snipers were waiting.

But Sunday brought a different story, one that "astonished" his team boss Frank Williams. Button made a lightning start to gain six places by the first corner, and it got better from there. Sound strategy and others' retirements elevated him to sixth and he was heading for a point in his first grand prix.

"Saturday was one of the worst days of my career," Button said. "But starting back there I was pretty relaxed."

Then he was awoken by the sound of a BMW engine going boom, and his car turned back into a pumpkin.

His barbs were as sharp as his driving and predictably sent McLaren boss Ron Dennis into rant mode [see sidebar]. But Schuey's gibes were less upsetting to him than the sight of Mika Hakkinen and David Coulthard grinding to a halt, each of them pluming a trail of engine smoke before the race was 20 laps old. What made it especially galling was that McLaren and engine supplier Mercedes had been focusing on reliability issues throughout the winter.

Mercedes motorsport chief Norbert Haug had no excuses, but was sanguine about the narrow performance gap between the top two teams. "I cannot expect Ferrari to be one second per lap slower every year," he said.

To accentuate the Mercedes PR disaster, Ralf Schumacher gave Williams's new partner [and Merc arch-rival] BMW a podium finish in its first grand prix since 1987.

In-between the Schumacher siblings, new Ferrari signing Rubens Barrichello proved to be his winning team-mate's closest rival. Schuey Snr wanted to put the newcomer in his place from day one, but in his anxiety to gain a psychological edge he stuck his car in the wall during free practice on Friday. Then, as the start lights went out, Schumacher moved abruptly across to cover Barrichello's start, which slowed Rubens and condemned him to spend some time behind Heinz-Harald Frentzen's Jordan.

Barrichello was far from spooked, however. He set the fastest lap during a mid-race charge in which he briefly overtook Schumacher, but the cheers that accompanied his moment in the spotlight were short-lived, because Ferrari had adjusted the Brazilian's strategy mid-race and he had an extra fuel stop to make.

DENNIS THE MENACED

AFTER A CALAMITOUS, POINTS-FREE 1999, BRITISH AMERICAN RACING BEGAN THE YEAR ON A BRIGHTER NOTE BY GETTING BOTH ITS CARS INTO THE TOP SIX

Sensing a chance to have a pop at the men in red, Dennis said the Brazilian was a "sacrificial lamb" who had no role other than to assist his team-mate's victory, but Ferrari technical director Ross Brawn defended his tactics. "Frentzen was holding us up," he said, "so we had nothing to lose and it was worth a punt. I'm not going to explain how our strategies work to Ron – he obviously doesn't understand them. I can only assume he is very upset about the performance of his own cars and he has become a bit irrational."

After a calamitous, points-free 1999, British American Racing began the year on a brighter note by getting both its cars into the top six. Jacques Villeneuve took fourth after leading a gaggle of cars round for much of the race. Ricardo Zonta finished seventh on the road, but inherited sixth from Mika Salo when the Finn was disqualified because his Sauber's front wing lacked the precision engineering one associates with certain Swiss-built products [clue: not racing cars].

The Jordans looked as if they could have threatened the Ferraris, but Frentzen and Jarno Trulli both retired when a top-three finish was feasible. It was tougher still, however, for "new" boy Jaguar [the team formerly known as Stewart, but now with full Ford control and a green paint job]. Its two cars had taken a tumble by lap five. Johnny Herbert described the weekend as his "worst three days ever". Team-mate Eddie Irvine, winner here a year earlier, preferred to change the subject and said: "McLaren are doing their best to throw it away again, aren't they?"

Maybe it was an innocent post-race comment. Perhaps it was just psychological nous. Whatever, Michael Schumacher's assertion that he would have won the Australian Grand Prix even if the two McLarens had made it to the finish was a red rag to the bullish Ron Dennis.

Momentarily, the McLaren boss dropped his customarily cool facade and hit back at the German, whose sentiments, he claimed, were "a load of rubbish".

"We outqualified Ferrari with both our cars," Dennis said. "We led comfortably from the start and were pulling away. Every lap we were setting a faster time than Schumacher. We had the race well in control, so for him to say he was just sitting there, waiting for us to fail, is ludicrous.

"There is no question that they have a good car, but to have the arrogance and pomposity to tell the world how wonderful you are is a waste of time. People might choose to buy into the hype and self-promotion, but let results be the judge."

Anyone with a McLaren-sensitive streak would be well advised at this point to fast-forward through the next couple of chapters and advance to the British GP at Silverstone, because Ron "I'll be judged by my results" Dennis was about to feel the force of a three-nil drubbing.

Ronsqueal: Dennis [above] was in a splendidly mard mood after the race. Above left, Villeneuve receives a hero's welcome after scoring his first points since Japan 1998

STARTING GRID

- **1 Hakkinen** 1m30.556s
- **2 Coulthard** 1m30.910s
- **3 M Schumacher** 1m31.075s
- **4 Barrichello** 1m31.102s
- **5 Frentzen** 1m31.359s
- **6 Trulli** 1m31.504s
- **7 Irvine** 1m31.514s
- **22 Villeneuve** 1m31.968s
- **11 Fisichella** 1m31.992s
- **17 Salo** 1m32.018s
- **9 R Schumacher** 1m32.220s
- **18 de la Rosa** 1m32.323s
- **19 Verstappen** 1m32.477s
- **12 Wurz** 1m32.775s
- **15 Heidfeld** 1m33.024s
- **23 Zonta** 1m33.117s
- **14 Alesi** 1m33.197s
- **20 Gené** 1m33.261s
- **16 Diniz** 1m33.378s
- **8 Herbert** 1m33.638s
- **10 Button** 1m33.828s
- **21 Mazzacane** 1m34.705s

March 12 2000
ALBERT PARK CIRCUIT, MELBOURNE
CIRCUIT LENGTH: 3.295miles / 5.303km

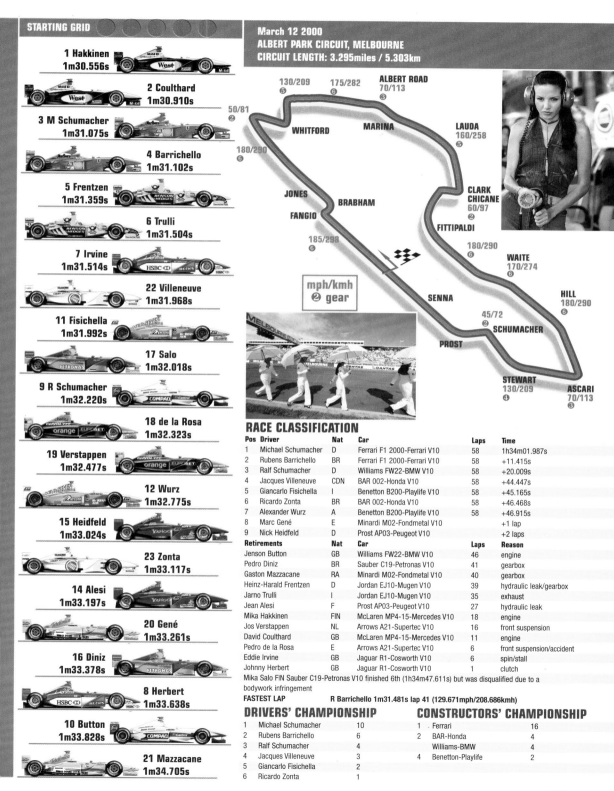

RACE CLASSIFICATION

Pos	Driver	Nat	Car	Laps	Time
1	Michael Schumacher	D	Ferrari F1 2000-Ferrari V10	58	1h34m01.987s
2	Rubens Barrichello	BR	Ferrari F1 2000-Ferrari V10	58	+11.415s
3	Ralf Schumacher	D	Williams FW22-BMW V10	58	+20.009s
4	Jacques Villeneuve	CDN	BAR 002-Honda V10	58	+44.447s
5	Giancarlo Fisichella	I	Benetton B200-Playlife V10	58	+45.165s
6	Ricardo Zonta	BR	BAR 002-Honda V10	58	+46.468s
7	Alexander Wurz	A	Benetton B200-Playlife V10	58	+46.915s
8	Marc Gené	E	Minardi M02-Fondmetal V10		+1 lap
9	Nick Heidfeld	D	Prost AP03-Peugeot V10		+2 laps

Retirements	Nat	Car	Laps	Reason
Jenson Button	GB	Williams FW22-BMW V10	46	engine
Pedro Diniz	BR	Sauber C19-Petronas V10	41	gearbox
Gaston Mazzacane	RA	Minardi M02-Fondmetal V10	40	gearbox
Heinz-Harald Frentzen	D	Jordan EJ10-Mugen V10	39	hydraulic leak/gearbox
Jarno Trulli	I	Jordan EJ10-Mugen V10	35	exhaust
Jean Alesi	F	Prost AP03-Peugeot V10	27	hydraulic leak
Mika Hakkinen	FIN	McLaren MP4-15-Mercedes V10	18	engine
Jos Verstappen	NL	Arrows A21-Supertec V10	16	front suspension
David Coulthard	GB	McLaren MP4-15-Mercedes V10	11	engine
Pedro de la Rosa	E	Arrows A21-Supertec V10	6	front suspension/accident
Eddie Irvine	GB	Jaguar R1-Cosworth V10	6	spin/stall
Johnny Herbert	GB	Jaguar R1-Cosworth V10	1	clutch

Mika Salo FIN Sauber C19-Petronas V10 finished 6th (1h34m47.611s) but was disqualified due to a bodywork infringement

FASTEST LAP   R Barrichello 1m31.481s lap 41 (129.671mph/208.686kmh)

DRIVERS' CHAMPIONSHIP

1	Michael Schumacher	10
2	Rubens Barrichello	6
3	Ralf Schumacher	4
4	Jacques Villeneuve	3
5	Giancarlo Fisichella	2
6	Ricardo Zonta	1

CONSTRUCTORS' CHAMPIONSHIP

1	Ferrari	16
2	BAR-Honda	4
	Williams-BMW	4
4	Benetton-Playlife	2

ONE STEP

AFTER THE PAINFU
LESSONS LEARNED
1999, GRAND PRIX RACING
NEWEST TEAM MADE
QUANTUM LEAP FORWAF
IN ITS SECOND SEASO
HERE'S THE INSIDE STORY C
BRITISH AMERICAN RACING
2000 CAMPAIG

BEYOND

Fourth road bridge: after a fallow 1999, Jacques Villeneuve [main shot] picked up a string of top-six finishes, without ever quite making the podium, to finish seventh in the 2000 world championship for drivers. Inset, Monza marked a landmark for engine partner Honda, which started its 200th grand prix

THERE ARE "LIES, DAMNED LIES, AND STATISTICS," AS THE SAYING GOES, BUT how about this for an interesting statistic? In 1998, the British American Racing-owned Tyrrell Formula One team had a top-10-finish-to-start ratio of 9.4 per cent. In 1999, British American Racing's first year of competition, that figure rose to 20.6 per cent. At the end of the 2000 season, BAR Honda's top-10 strike rate was 50 per cent.

Much has been written during the last three years about the progress and the politics of F1's youngest and – arguably – most ambitious team, but that statistic in many ways encapsulates the most important story concerning BAR. That can be summed up in one word – progress.

In the last decade, 13 truly new teams have launched themselves expectantly into the ultra-competitive arena of the F1 world championship. Of those, nine have fallen by the wayside and one has metamorphosed into a different team.

In short, the odds of a new team surviving in the F1 jungle, let alone of achieving success, are not likely to be a punter's delight. And the ever-escalating financial costs and mind-boggling technical demands of the sport make it more difficult for new teams to join the fray with each succeeding year.

Add to that the fact that the FIA [the governing body of world motor sport] has decided to limit the grid to 12 two-car teams, and it becomes clear why F1 is the world's most exclusive and challenging sport. It is also why BAR's performance this year has been particularly creditable.

After the disappointment – or "reality check", as managing director Craig Pollock termed it – of its first season of competition, which resulted in BAR becoming the undisputed holder of F1's wooden spoon, the team went back to the drawing board in several ways during the winter break.

When it re-emerged in its 2000 guise late in January, gone was the controversial split-livery design that had adorned the BAR cars and uniforms the previous year. An altogether neater, more corporate look replaced it, featuring a primarily white car carrying Lucky Strike's distinctive bull's-eye logo.

Also missing at the launch in London were comments concerning the likelihood of race wins that had led to media criticism the previous year. The Pollock "reality check" extended to all aspects of the team, including its expectations, and the new look was in many ways an outward indication of a fresh start.

The team's new chassis, the BAR 002, was what technical director Malcolm Oastler described as "evolutionary rather than revolutionary". The team's 1999 contender had shown flashes of real speed, but had often suffered from mechanical reliability problems. When it came to the new car, Oastler and chief designer Andy Green concentrated on consolidating the technical lessons learned the previous season and addressing reliability, while aiming to make significant performance gains.

Strengthening their hand were two important new cards they had been dealt. In May 1999, Japanese giant Honda announced it was returning to F1 after a gap of seven years and would be the official engine supplier and exclusive technical partner of BAR.

What this meant in practical terms was that BAR would be supplied with Honda's compact, powerful RA000E V10 engine for the 2000 season. Equally significantly, Honda chiefs had decided that the company's third era of F1 participation would involve its engineers in a test and development programme extending to such areas as suspension design, aerodynamics and advanced chassis control systems.

The appearance of Honda's "Athena" car at a Nogaro test in late May was the first tangible evidence of this technical co-operation. As the season progressed, the chassis, a joint BAR-Honda development, ran alongside the team's two normal test machines and provided a platform for Honda engineers to put their latest ideas on F1 hardware and software to the test.

A new wind tunnel was the second ace in BAR's hand. Tucked away behind the main Brackley factory, the eagerly awaited facility opened its doors officially on February 7 and was running flat out within a matter of weeks. Aerodynamics remains one of the key technical areas where it is possible to make significant performance gains in modern

THERE WERE SMILES AND TEARS IN EQUAL MEASURE AFTER THE CHEQUERED FLAG HAD FALLEN. BAR WAS FINALLY ON THE F1 SCOREBOARD

Mumble in the jungle: despite BAR's conspicuous progress, things didn't always go to plan. Main shot, Villeneuve takes the long way home. Below, from the top: celebrating points in Melbourne; technical director Malcolm Oastler [to the left] with team boss Craig Pollock; not the only thing Ricardo Zonta ran into during the season

F1. It is essential for any serious team to have its own wind tunnel in order to ensure sustained aero development.

BAR's ranks up there with those of the best teams in the sport and the increased competitiveness of the BAR-Honda 002 in the latter part of the season was due, at least in part, to the hard work of the aerodynamics department.

In the curtain-raising Australian Grand Prix, the team opened its account in fine style. Drivers Jacques Villeneuve and Ricardo Zonta claimed fourth and sixth and, at a stroke, relegated the unpleasant memories of the previous year to the motor racing history books.

It was an emotional moment for those who had brought the BAR dream to fruition only two years previously. It wasn't too surprising, then, that the combination of relief and happiness at the points-scoring performance meant there were smiles and tears in equal measure after the chequered flag had fallen. BAR was finally on the F1 scoreboard and there was everything to play for.

As with any racing season, there were ups and downs. After the euphoria of Australia, Brazil brought a reality check of its own as Villeneuve failed to finish and Zonta came home 10th. In the first European round of the world championship, Imola's San Marino GP, Villeneuve translated a blindingly fast start – one of his trademarks throughout the season – into a fifth-place finish courtesy of some fine pit work and good strategy. Zonta, too, looked to be on course for a top-10 result, but a broken exhaust put paid to his efforts and he eventually finished 12th.

There followed what might best be described as a mid-season stumble, and it wasn't until the French GP, at the beginning of July, that the team appeared to regain its composure. Following an excellent fourth place at Magny-Cours, Villeneuve reeled off four points-scoring results in the remaining eight rounds and was a genuine podium candidate at Monza – an electronic problem put paid to that – and arguably a contender in America and Malaysia.

Zonta, too, had his moments – particularly in the Italian GP. Starting 17th, he carved his way through the field in electrifying fashion after being forced to pit at the end of the first lap to replace a punctured tyre. He made two further, scheduled pit stops, both beautifully executed, and pounded home sixth.

As one expects in motor racing, there were low spots, too, notably in Monaco, where the team struggled for pace even though Villeneuve finished a frustrated seventh, just out of the points. He also missed a scoring opportunity at his home race, in

Montreal, because of unpredictable weather and a pit stop mix-up.

For Zonta, the season undoubtedly hit rock bottom at the German GP, when what looked like another double points-scoring opportunity yielded only an eighth place for Villeneuve. This was the consequence of an incident between the BAR team-mates on lap 34. Villeneuve spun but recovered, while Zonta crashed out for good within four laps. Little more than two weeks later, the team announced that it had signed experienced French driver, and former GP winner, Olivier Panis to replace Zonta in 2001.

The United States GP at the famed Indianapolis Motor Speedway was possibly the best race of the year for the team. The event marked the return of F1 to the US after a nine-year absence and Villeneuve, a former winner of the world-famous Indianapolis 500, was understandably in constant demand by the American media during the build-up.

The race turned out to be one of the most intriguing of the season and, as it unfolded, Villeneuve and Zonta were in the thick of the action. When, after 73 laps, their cars crossed the famous line of bricks that denotes the start-finish, Villeneuve was fourth and Zonta sixth.

For a brief, euphoric moment close to the end, it had looked as though the hard-charging Villeneuve might grab BAR-Honda's first-ever podium finish as he battled with Heinz-Harald Frentzen's Jordan. Unfortunately for the 1997 world champion, a bold outbraking manoeuvre didn't pay off and, although he hounded Frentzen during the closing laps, he wasn't able to force the German into a mistake.

But BAR's sophomore season was about more than just results. On the plus side, there were the efforts of BAR's test team and drivers Darren Manning and Patrick Lemarié. Their schedule was often as busy as that of the race crew and, under the guidance of

COLLECTIVELY THE TEAM SHRUGGED OFF ITS DETRACTORS, REMAINED FOCUSED ON THE BUSINESS OF RACING AND MADE TANGIBLE PROGRESS

A wish called Honda, clockwise from top left: Zonta zips along at Monza; Villeneuve sneaked off between races to take part in cult darts quiz *Bullseye* and won himself a speedboat; Zonta and mates commute to Hockenheim — not sure if it's through the pre-race rainwater or Barrichello's post-race tears; BAR pit drill perked up in 2000; Barrichello and Hakkinen follow Villeneuve, who ran as high as second in Canada before launching an Exocet attack on Ralf Schumacher

newly appointed test team manager Andrew Alsworth, they undoubtedly made a significant contribution to BAR's overall performance.

Also in the good news column, Jacques Villeneuve committed himself to three more years with the team, confounding F1 pundits who were convinced the Quebec-born star would part company with BAR. "We are absolutely delighted with Jacques' decision and the fact he has registered a significant vote of confidence in British American Racing," Craig Pollock said as the news was announced. "Jacques has been an integral part of the team since its formation two years ago. His commitment to stay indicates that he shares our belief that this is an organisation with which he can win races and, ultimately, the world championship."

On the downside, Ricardo Zonta experienced a pair of frightening, high-speed crashes in testing, at Silverstone and Monza. Mercifully he emerged unscathed, but the young Brazilian freely admitted the accidents had given his confidence a knock. With a racing driver's sang froid, however, he explained that he was able to reconcile both incidents in his mind since they were the result of specific technical problems, for which the reasons were understood.

Sadly, BAR lost one of its original sponsors, Teleglobe. The Canadian-based company decided to leave the world of F1 after its sale to telecommunications giant BCE produced a predictable change in marketing priorities. Before the season was over, however, the team gained three significant new backers – World Online, Bee-Trade.com and ART [Advanced Research Technologies] – to complement the existing line-up of BAT/Lucky Strike, Sonax, K-Way/Multimoda Network, Koni and Technogym.

Overall, 2000 has to rate as a highly constructive year for BAR – one in which the team came of age. Yes, rumour and speculation continued to swirl around at various times, but collectively the team shrugged off its detractors, remained focused on the business of racing and made tangible progress. In so doing, it established itself as one of the best of the rest, behind F1's recognised top two. It laid solid foundations for what is intended to be a long and successful involvement in the sport.

"To have finished equal on points with Benetton this year in the world championship for constructors and stayed well ahead of Jordan is tremendous," Pollock said immediately after the Malaysian GP. "It's a perfect end to the season and as much as we could have reasonably expected to accomplish in our second year. I am so proud of everyone, both here and back at the factory."

On the Monday morning after the race, following a 12-hour, overnight flight from Kuala Lumpur and a 60-minute dash by road, Pollock went straight to the factory floor at Brackley to thank every member of the team personally for a job well done. F1 might be widely regarded as the ultimate high-technology sport, but as BAR's managing director clearly indicated, no team can expect to move forward without human endeavour.

GRANDE PREMIO MARLBORO DO BRASI

HE MIGHT HAVE BEEN PREVENTED FROM TAKING A SHOT AT POLE BY A BLEND OF COMEDY BRAZILIAN CARPENTRY AND BAD WEATHER, BUT THERE WAS NOTHING TO IMPEDE SCHUEY IN THE RACE

Forward pass: Stan Laurel (above) slices inside leader Hakkinen before romping away with the Brazilian GP. Further back, Coulthard – note the front wing that's 7mm too low – fights to repel Barrichello

IF YOU WERE IN ANY DOUBT WHOSE SIDE THE CROWD WAS ON, YOU ONLY HAD to look at two miles of humanity queuing to get in at 7.30 on race day morning. It was a sea of purest red, but for the occasional smattering of national flags [Brazilian, of course].

The nation had always dreamed of seeing its late icon Ayrton Senna bedecked in scarlet, but this was the next best thing. Fresh from a strong showing in Australia, Rubens Barrichello was the first home driver ever to race an F1 Ferrari at Interlagos – and with it he became the biggest catalyst in history for sales of bootleg team merchandise. As far as the fans were concerned, no one else mattered.

Michael Schumacher admitted that Barrichello was closer to his pace than Eddie Irvine had ever been. More's the pity, then, that Barrichello succumbed to a rare Ferrari reliability failure at half-distance and left Schumacher to romp to his second straight victory.

Having lost out in qualifying [see sidebar], the Ferraris were put on a two-stop strategy and profited from their light fuel load by overtaking the McLarens within the first couple of laps. Schumacher passed both his silver rivals and Barrichello duped Coulthard twice.

So far so good – but it then took Barrichello 14 laps to get past Hakkinen, and by then Schuey was long gone. When Rubens quit with hydraulic failure 10 laps later, many of the crowd decided it was time for them to pack up and leave, too.

Ferrari technical director Ross Brawn said: "We had nothing to lose – following McLaren all race wouldn't have got us anywhere. Having opted for a two-stop strategy, it was essential that we passed the McLarens at the beginning. Michael managed but it took Rubens a while longer."

The Ferraris had plenty of time to make up in order to allow for a second stop, so the issue wasn't really settled until Hakkinen toured in on lap 30 to complain he had no power. With Coulthard's gearbox playing up prior to his eventual disqualification [see sidebar], it was to be Schumacher's day. The seasonal tally made McLaren's defence look worse than Oxford United's – Schumacher 20, Ron Dennis's blokes 0.

THE FERRARIS HAD PLENTY OF TIME TO MAKE UP IN ORDER TO ALLOW FOR A SECOND STOP, UNTIL HAKKINEN TOURED IN ON LAP 30 TO COMPLAIN HE HAD NO POWER

Every Brazilian GP winner since 1994 has gone on to take the world title, but Schumacher didn't want to hear such talk.

"I was told that whoever wins the first race wins the championship," he said, dismissively. "Now they tell me whoever wins in Brazil wins the championship. Perhaps that means I can go home and not bother driving for the rest of the year."

It was, of course, a load of spherical nonsense. And speaking of which... Pele – who might be good enough to make the England side even today – presented Schuey with his winner's trophy and the discourse, according to a badly scripted press release went something like this...

Schumacher and Pele had a good humorated [sic] conversation that began with the driver's affirmation: "I can also to [sic] a good job with a ball."

Scarlet fever: Rubens Barrichello was the first Brazilian to race an F1 Ferrari at home – and fans turned up in force (above). They waved their (mostly contraband) flags especially hard when Rubinho passed Hakkinen (far right), but cleared off when his Ferrari faltered. Button (right) scored his first point

A BANNER IN THE WORKS

Qualifying in Brazil turned up a surprise winner – not Hakkinen or Schumacher, but Morris. Philip Morris, that is.

The parent company of fag maker Marlboro earned itself 30 minutes of global publicity when three of its advertising hoardings fell down along Interlagos's main straight during the session, which was broadcast live on TV all over the world. There were considerable delays as a result – and the level of exposure accrued by Marlboro made a mockery of any attempt to reduce tobacco advertising in the sport.

After the third and final interruption, when a hoarding hit Jean Alesi's Prost, the clouds opened and the session was washed out. For once, Marlboro had done ex-partner McLaren a favour by leaving Hakkinen and Coulthard on the front row, despite Ferrari having threatened to go quicker.

After initial reports of sabotage, the race organiser revealed: "The force of the wind on the main straight broke the nylon ties, which have previously proven to be resistant and adequate for this type of structure."

The errant boards were removed in time for Sunday's race. The normally fiery Alesi, meanwhile, was surprisingly restrained after being hit on the head at 180mph.

"It was dangerous and I'm annoyed, but it wasn't intentional," he said. "It was a stupid accident which could have been very serious. But they just don't have the money to do everything that needs doing here."

Two weeks later Interlagos had even less money after being fined to the tune of £60,000 by the FIA. Somebody should have seen the signs.

WING LOW, SWEET CHARIOT

It never rains for David Coulthard, but it certainly pours. The Scotsman came into the season determined to turn around his two-year losing streak against team-mate Mika Hakkinen.

Gone, we were told, would be the Mr Nice Guy approach. In came a new routine of fitness training with a side salad of extra steel.

An engine problem had put paid to his efforts in Australia, but this time DC appeared to have got things right. Robbed of second and third gears early in the race, he wrestled his car to the flag and six hard-earned points. Mercedes boss Norbert Haug later described David's race as "the finest of his career".

His points, however, lasted for all of three hours. After that, word filtered out that the front wing of his McLaren was too low by 7mm, which is just outside the FIA's permitted 5mm tolerance.

Immediately McLaren lodged an appeal and claimed the car had suffered structural damage because of the bumpy circuit. The appeal was heard a week later – and McLaren lost.

Perhaps team boss Ron Dennis might regret comments made after Sauber's withdrawal on Saturday, when he said: "We've measured the bumps and are pretty comfortable that we've got it handled. The challenge of going F1 racing is making your car strong and reliable enough to finish."

Next time, Ron, try building it to the right dimensions, too.

Poisoned Arrows: Verstappen flew in the early stages (above left) – until his neck became sore and he dropped out of the top six. Runner-up Fisichella prepares to pounce. Above, Coulthard practises for a role in Ibiza Uncovered by necking a pint of Mumm in four seconds flat

JENSON BUTTON BECAME THE FIRST EMBRYO EVER TO SCORE A WORLD CHAMPIONSHIP POINT, AND IN ONLY HIS SECOND RACE

The answer of Pele was that he had heard before that Schumacher used to play with balls. "I want to play with you sometime. We have to set a date very quickly," he said.

Giancarlo Fisichella, who was also on the podium, pointed out that he was a better footballer than Schuey [although he'd obviously risk smashing his sunglasses if he played]. The Italian proved that he wasn't a bad driver, either, by finishing third on the road and second in the FIA's logbook during the week that former boss Flavio Briatore regained control of Benetton on behalf of his new employer Renault.

Behind Fisico were two Jordans and two Williams-BMWs – which meant that Jenson Button became the first embryo ever to score a world championship point, and in only his second race, too. Despite making "my worst start ever", the Englishman had a dream day and eventually secured the final top-six berth after passing Jos Verstappen's Arrows.

After a magnificent first stint, the Dutchman ran as high as third before his fitness let him down. "My neck was gone," he said. "The first part of the race was unbelievably good but I couldn't handle the second half. I was tired, everything hurt and I was totally finished."

Worse still for Verstappen, the prescribed medicine was a workout session with team owner Tom Walkinshaw's other hobby, aka Gloucester Rugby Football Club.

As for Jaguar, Johnny Herbert took one further than it had ever gone before [ie he didn't retire until the 53rd lap]. That was better than Sauber managed – the cars of Mika Salo and Pedro Diniz suffered rear wing failures in practice and were withdrawn from the race as a result. Strangely, loads of Brazilians thought it worth turning up on Sunday, despite the mighty Pedro's absence.

STARTING GRID

1 Hakkinen
1m14.111s

2 Coulthard
1m14.285s

3 M Schumacher
1m14.508s

4 Barrichello
1m14.636s

11 Fisichella
1m15.375s

7 Irvine
1m15.425s

5 Frentzen
1m15.455s

23 Zonta
1m15.484s

10 Button
1m15.490s

22 Villeneuve
1m15.515s

9 R Schumacher
1m15.561s

6 Trulli
1m15.627s

12 Wurz
1m15.664s

19 Verstappen
1m15.704s

14 Alesi
1m15.715s

18 de la Rosa
1m16.002s

8 Herbert
1m16.250s

20 Gené
1m16.380s

15 Heidfeld
1m17.112s

21 Mazzacane
1m17.512s

17 Pedro Diniz BR qualified 20th (1m17.178s) and
16 Mika Salo FIN qualified 22nd (1m18.703s), but they were
withdrawn by Sauber because of rear wing failures

March 26 2000
AUTODROMO JOSÉ CARLOS PACE, INTERLAGOS, SÃO PAULO
CIRCUIT LENGTH: 2.677miles/4.309km

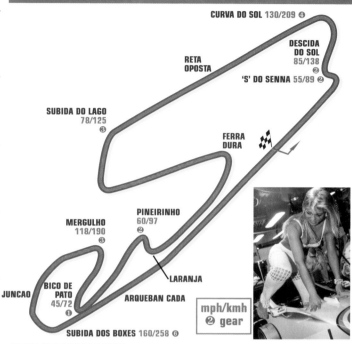

CURVA DO SOL 130/209 ➍

DESCIDA DO SOL 85/138 ➐

RETA OPOSTA

'S' DO SENNA 55/89 ➋

SUBIDA DO LAGO 78/125 ➌

FERRA DURA

PINEIRINHO 60/97 ➋

MERGULHO 118/190 ➌

LARANJA

BICO DE PATO 45/72 ➊

JUNCAO

ARQUEBAN CADA

mph/kmh
➋ gear

SUBIDA DOS BOXES 160/258 ➏

RACE CLASSIFICATION

Pos	Driver	Nat	Car	Laps	Time
1	Michael Schumacher	D	Ferrari F1 2000-Ferrari V10	71	1h31m35.271s
2	Giancarlo Fisichella	I	Benetton B200-Playlife V10	71	+39.898s
3	Heinz-Harald Frentzen	D	Jordan EJ10-Mugen V10	71	+42.268s
4	Jarno Trulli	I	Jordan EJ10-Mugen V10	71	+1m12.780s
5	Ralf Schumacher	D	Williams FW22-BMW V10		+1 lap
6	Jenson Button	GB	Williams FW22-BMW V10		+1 lap
7	Jos Verstappen	NL	Arrows A21-Supertec V10		+1 lap
8	Pedro de la Rosa	E	Arrows A21-Supertec V10		+1 lap
9	Ricardo Zonta	BR	BAR 002-Honda V10		+2 laps
10	Gaston Mazzacane	RA	Minardi M02-Fondmetal V10		+2 laps

Retirements	Nat	Car	Laps	Reason
Johnny Herbert	GB	Jaguar R1-Cosworth V10	51	gearbox
Marc Gené	E	Minardi M02-Fondmetal V10	31	engine
Mika Hakkinen	FIN	McLaren MP4-15-Mercedes V10	30	oil pressure
Rubens Barrichello	BR	Ferrari F1 2000-Ferrari V10	27	hydraulics
Eddie Irvine	GB	Jaguar R1-Cosworth V10	20	accident
Jacques Villeneuve	CDN	BAR 002-Honda V10	16	gearbox
Jean Alesi	F	Prost AP03-Peugeot V10	11	electronics
Nick Heidfeld	D	Prost AP03-Peugeot V10	9	engine
Alexander Wurz	A	Benetton B200-Playlife V10	7	engine

FASTEST LAP   **M Schumacher 1m14.755s lap 48 (128.941mph/207.510kmh)**

David Coulthard   GB   McLaren MP4-15-Mercedes V10, finished 2nd (+4.302s) but was
disqualified due to the front wing end plates being lower than permitted.

DRIVERS' CHAMPIONSHIP

1	Michael Schumacher	20
2	Giancarlo Fisichella	8
3	Rubens Barrichello	6
	Ralf Schumacher	6
5	Heinz-Harald Frentzen	4
6	Jarno Trulli	3
	Jacques Villeneuve	3
8	Jenson Button	1
	Ricardo Zonta	1

CONSTRUCTORS' CHAMPIONSHIP

1	Ferrari	26
2	Benetton-Playlife	8
3	Jordan-Mugen	7
	Williams-BMW	7
5	BAR-Honda	4

200 STYLES PER HOUR

"SHE'S A MODEL AND SHE'S LOOKING GOOD," WARBLED ELECTRO-TEUTONS KRAFTWERK BACK IN 1978. THEY RELEASED "THE MODEL" ON 12-INCH FLUORESCENT VINYL IN SEPTEMBER OF THAT YEAR AND THUS IT USUALLY GOT PLAYED AT ABOUT THREE IN THE MORNING. DAFT? YES – BUT NO MORE SO THAN SOME OF THE STUFF THAT GOES ON IN F1 PADDOCKS NOWADAYS

Almost bare necessities: wherever this was taken [far left], it clearly wasn't Silverstone or the Nürburgring or they'd have turned blue and yellow. Will these be comfortable when you sit down to lunch [centre left, top]? No, frankly. Williams and BMW nicked a load of lab technicians' coats for PR purposes [centre left, below], in the belief that this was more fetching than a spray-on yellow bikini. A poor fit [left] – or proof that waifs Jacques Villeneuve and Ricardo Zonta are fatter than the average supermodel. If they smoked what they were advertising, their teeth wouldn't be that white [below left]. Extras from a James Bond movie featuring some improbable, but nonetheless watchable, space-station nonsense [bottom left]. Token shot selected by the art editor because he has a penchant for blondes [below right]. BAR made several steps forward this year – but didn't teach some members of the team vital lessons about looking the right way [far left, below]

GRAN PREMIO WARSTEINER DI SAN MARINO

IN FRONT OF SEVERAL MILLION
PEOPLE SPORTING RED T-SHIRTS
AND DAFT HAIR DYE, SCHUEY
SURVIVES A CLOSE ENCOUNTER OF
THE NERD KIND WITH THE WANDERING
PEDRO DINIZ AND RACKS UP A
THIRD STRAIGHT SUCCESS

Smugshot: one of these men has just won a grand
prix (above), the other is a massively hacked-off Finn.
Below, partial marshals do their best to mimic
a crowd that's about to treble the Peroni brewery's
annual turnover

MIKA HAKKINEN CLINCHED HIS THIRD STRAIGHT POLE POSITION AT IMOLA – but Michael Schumacher squashed the McLarens once again to take his third straight success.

McLaren had everything it needed to score its first win of the year. Its MP4-15 just about had the edge on Ferrari's F1-2000 and Hakkinen was on the kind of form that usually makes him an irresistible adversary, but a combination of inferior tactics and a momentary electronic glitch combined to give Schuey a hat trick.

At least Hakkinen and David Coulthard trailed home in second and third, to give McLaren some legitimate points, but it was the first time since 1976 [with Niki Lauda and Clay Regazzoni] that Ferrari had won the opening three grands prix of the season. The last time the same driver won the opening three grands prix of a campaign for the Prancing Horse had been in 1953, courtesy of Alberto Ascari. [Please don't write in to point out that, actually, he only won three of the first four championship events that season, because America's Indianapolis 500 counted towards the title. We know – but it wasn't an F1 GP and neither Ascari nor Ferrari was there.]

It was also Schumacher's 16th grand prix success in a Ferrari, which put him ahead of Lauda in Ferrari's list of all-time world championship grand prix winners. He still had some way to go to catch Ascari, however, because the chubby Italian won 37 top-class single-seater races for the men in red – it's just that there weren't as many championship events back when Brylcreem was all the rage and Elvis had still to be invented.

It was always clear that this would be a close fight. Schumacher felt – with justification – that he could have shaded Mika for pole. It might have helped, however, had he not mistakenly flicked on the pit lane speed limiter as he came through Rivazza on one of his qualifying runs. He didn't admit to that one...

Come the race, Hakkinen made the best start – and Schuey made enemies. While the Finn zapped away, the German had to weave to keep the quicker-starting Coulthard at bay

A COMBINATION OF INFERIOR TACTICS AND A MOMENTARY ELECTRONIC GLITCH COMBINED TO GIVE SCHUEY A HAT TRICK

and slowed the Scot sufficiently to push him back behind Ferrari number two Rubens Barrichello. This was to ruin David's afternoon. The Brazilian might have run relatively close to his team-mate in the opening two races, but Hakkinen wasn't a factor to the end on either occasion. Here, when Michael had to push 100 per cent all the way, Barrichello was left far behind – and DC was stuck behind him until he pulled off the only significant physical passing manoeuvre of the afternoon when the pair left the pits at the end of their second round of scheduled stops.

It was the second round of stops that did for Hakkinen, too. Having led comfortably from the start, McLaren sent him out for relatively short, 17-lap middle stint. At the first round of stops, Schuey took on a bit more fuel that kept him stationary for an extra second but gave him four more laps of track time.

At one point during that second part of the race, the Finn had pulled out a lead of almost five seconds. By the time he stopped,

Pit flop: McLaren's perennially questionable tactics weren't all that different to Ferrari's, but Hakkinen lost the race after his second scheduled stop [above]. Chop Schuey: Michael's dubious getaway tactics [right] send his brother Ralf temporarily onto the grass and force Coulthard to slow sufficiently allow the steam-powered Barrichello through

TRADING PLACES

At Imola in 1999, Nick Heidfeld [left, above] won the opening round of the FIA Formula 3000 Championship on the Saturday afternoon before the San Marino Grand Prix. It had been the springboard to a successful title campaign that eventually helped him clinch his F1 dream.

Unfortunately for the Mercedes-backed German, there were only lean pickings available when it came to signing an F1 deal. His backer had Hakkinen and Coulthard on its books, so there was no space at McLaren. Sauber was very keen on his services, but couldn't clinch a deal, and then there was Prost...

This was supposed to be a fresh start for the French team at the beginning of its final year with engine partner Peugeot. It had the most experienced driver in the field, in Jean Alesi, and a new boy whose pedigree marked him out as a future champion.

At Imola, however, Heidfeld – who had received precious little track time because his car kept breaking – lined up 22nd and last, fractionally behind the sweet-handling but underpowered Minardis.

He finally got the car working in the warm-up... but then it died on the grid. It was eventually persuaded to start and his lap times in the race were decent – but you needed a digital TV monitor to be aware of as much. The AP03 expired with hyraulics failure after 22 laps and, five minutes later, Alesi's car conked out with a similar malfunction. At least Heidfeld knew he was getting parity of equipment.

While his reputation was getting a mauling, however, there was a certain irony in the fact that Olivier Panis [right, above] – dumped by Prost in 1999 – was reviving his own career by doing some sterling work in Heidfeld's old job, as a McLaren tester.

SCHUMACHER EMERGED SLIGHTLY AHEAD OF THE FINN FOR THE FIRST TIME – AND OVERTAKING IS NOT MUCH OF AN OPTION AT IMOLA. IT WAS GAME OVER

however, Schuey had reduced his arrears to 1.6 seconds, not least because Mika's engine suddenly cut at one point. "It was as though someone in the crowd had switched me off," he said. In fact, a power spike caused his transmission to select neutral – and fishing for a gear cost him about 2.5 seconds.

That was offset slightly because Schuey lost time lapping the Sauber of Pedro Diniz, who tried to be helpful but achieved the opposite affect because he didn't anticipate what a proper racing driver would do in the circumstances. Hakkinen pitted for the last time on lap 44, Schuey on lap 48. The vital difference was that each of the Ferrari star's extra laps was pure dynamite – and his second stop was, of course, slightly shorter than Hakkinen's because he needed less fuel. He emerged slightly ahead of the Finn for the first time – and overtaking is not much of an option at Imola. It was game over.

By the end Coulthard was almost a minute in arrears thanks to Ferrari's jammer car. And that was as much as he had lost by following him during the first two stints. In the final 16 laps, he left the Brazilian more than half a minute behind.

Fifth went to Jacques Villeneuve, who profited from the knock-on effect of Schuey's first-lap weaving to spring from ninth on the grid, and the dependable Mika Salo claimed the final point for Sauber. The only race worth watching, however, had been that at the front.

CRUEL FOR CATS

Eddie Irvine cemented his place in history at Imola, by becoming the first man in history to finish a Formula One race in a Jaguar. About half a minute later, his team-mate Johnny Herbert became the second man to accomplish such a feat.

The first two races brought little joy for the Ford-owned team – particularly in Australia, where there had been a huge PR spend to fly in guests who watched the cars last at least a couple of minutes.

San Marino brought hope, however. Irvine lined up seventh but, as was always the case with the Jag in the first half of the season, made an awful start because of a clutch problem. Even so, he ran ahead of a group of cars that included sixth-placed finisher Mika Salo, but a misfire set in before the end and dropped him to the back of the train to rob him of the marque's first point.

Still, the Ulsterman was impressed, having chased hard after Jarno Trulli's Jordan until the Italian dropped out close to the end.

The sense of optimism was a pleasant contrast to some of the hot air there had been at the start of the year about the Big Cats being Back. It was sharp marketing-speak, but a little hard to accept because they had never been in grand prix racing in the first place. They were very good at Le Mans in the Fifties, late Eighties and early Nineties, sure, but the firm's previous F1 pedigree was an exact match for that of Reliant, Moskvich or Wartburg.

Imola marked a modest step forward, but a step forward nonetheless.

Plucky strike: [above left] Villeneuve made the most of a gift start to add another top-six finish to BAR's collection. Above, Salo and Irvine contemplate the dual miracles of a) not being excluded for once and b) a race that lasted longer than five laps

STARTING GRID

1 Hakkinen
1m24.714s

3 M Schumacher
1m24.805s

2 Coulthard
1m25.014s

4 Barrichello
1m25.242s

9 R Schumacher
1m25.871s

5 Frentzen
1m25.892s

7 Irvine
1m25.929s

6 Trulli
1m26.002s

22 Villeneuve
1m26.124s

16 Diniz
1m26.238s

12 Wurz
1m26.281s

17 Salo
1m26.336s

18 de la Rosa
1m26.349s

23 Zonta
1m26.814s

14 Alesi
1m26.824s

19 Verstappen
1m26.845s

8 Herbert
1m27.051s

10 Button
1m27.135s

11 Fisichella
1m27.253s

21 Mazzacane
1m28.161s

20 Gené
1m28.333s

15 Heidfeld
1m28.361s

April 9 2000
AUTODROMO ENZO E DINO FERRARI, IMOLA
CIRCUIT LENGTH: 3.065miles / 4.933km

mph/kmh
② gear

TOSA 55/89 ②

PIRATELLA 105/169 ④

VILLENEUVE 85/137 ③

175/281 ⑥

ACQUE MINERALE 70/113 ③

TAMBURELLO 100/161 ③

VARIANTE ALTA 75/121 ③

TRAGUARDO 55/89 ②

RIVAZZA 65/105 ②

VARIANTE BASSA 180/290 ③

RACE CLASSIFICATION

Pos	Driver	Nat	Car	Laps	Time
1	Michael Schumacher	D	Ferrari F1 2000-Ferrari V10	62	1h31m39.776s
2	Mika Hakkinen	FIN	McLaren MP4-15-Mercedes V10	62	+1.168s
3	David Coulthard	GB	McLaren MP4-15-Mercedes V10	62	+51.008s
4	Rubens Barrichello	BR	Ferrari F1 2000-Ferrari V10	62	+1m29.276s
5	Jacques Villeneuve	CDN	BAR 002-Honda V10		+1 lap
6	Mika Salo	FIN	Sauber C19-Petronas V10		+1 lap
7	Eddie Irvine	GB	Jaguar R1-Cosworth V10		+1 lap
8	Pedro Diniz	BR	Sauber C19-Petronas V10		+1 lap
9	Alexander Wurz	A	Benetton B200-Playlife V10		+1 lap
10	Johnny Herbert	GB	Jaguar R1-Cosworth V10		+1 lap
11	Giancarlo Fisichella	I	Benetton B200-Playlife V10		+1 lap
12	Ricardo Zonta	BR	BAR 002-Honda V10		+1 lap
13	Gaston Mazzacane	RA	Minardi M02-Fondmetal V10		+2 laps
14	Jos Verstappen	NL	Arrows A21-Supertec V10		+3 laps
15	Jarno Trulli	I	Jordan EJ10-Mugen V10		+4 laps
Retirements		**Nat**	**Car**	**Laps**	**Reason**
Pedro de la Rosa		E	Arrows A21-Supertec V10	49	gear selection/spin
Ralf Schumacher		D	Williams FW22-BMW V10	45	fuel pump
Jean Alesi		F	Prost AP03-Peugeot V10	25	hydraulic pressure/throttle
Nick Heidfeld		D	Prost AP03-Peugeot V10	22	hydraulic pressure
Jenson Button		GB	Williams FW22-BMW V10	5	engine
Marc Gené		E	Minardi M02-Fondmetal V10	5	spin
Heinz-Harald Frentzen		D	Jordan EJ10-Mugen V10	4	gear selection

FASTEST LAP M Hakkinen 1m26.523s lap 60 (127.536mph/205.249kmh)

DRIVERS' CHAMPIONSHIP

1	Michael Schumacher	30
2	Rubens Barrichello	9
3	Giancarlo Fisichella	8
4	Mika Hakkinen	6
	Ralf Schumacher	6
6	Jacques Villeneuve	5
7	David Coulthard	4
	Heinz-Harald Frentzen	4
9	Jarno Trulli	3
10	Jenson Button	1
	Mika Salo	1
	Ricardo Zonta	1

CONSTRUCTORS' CHAMPIONSHIP

1	Ferrari	39
2	McLaren-Mercedes	10
3	Benetton-Playlife	8
4	Jordan-Mugen	7
	Williams-BMW	7
6	BAR-Honda	6
7	Sauber-Petronas	1

WIN A DAY AT THE HEART

Grand prix motor racing is renowned as a secretive business, where rival teams do their best to keep each other off the scent of latest developments. For the public, too, it's often a mysterious business, conducted beyond tall security fences and behind closed doors. But now, thanks to British American Racing, you could get a first-hand glimpse of what makes a modern F1 team tick. We are offering one lucky winner and his or her guest the chance to join BAR for a test day at Silverstone in 2001.

This is the bit you don't see on TV – top teams preparing for life at the cutting edge every other Sunday. You'll be able to watch the cars in action, visit the pit garage, talk to team members and enjoy a relaxing lunch... just about everything short of driving the car, in fact.

For a chance to win this once in a lifetime opportunity, simply answer the following five questions correctly and send your entry on a postcard to: Hazleton Publishing Ltd, 3 Richmond Hill, Richmond, Surrey TW10 6RE, to arrive no later than first post on Monday, January 31, 2001.

The first all-correct entry to be drawn wins the prize.
Good luck [and, if you win, remember to take some earplugs].

OF FORMULA ONE

QUESTIONS

1 WHAT IS INCOMING BAR DRIVER OLIVIER PANIS'S MAIN CLAIM TO FAME?

A) He scored the Ligier F1 team's final grand prix win, at Monaco in 1996

B) He scored the winning try for France against Wales in a Home International rugby fixture in 1997

C) When he's not driving a GP car his main hobby is flower arranging

2 IN WHICH COUNTRY IS THE HOST GP TRACK NAMED AFTER BAR STAR JACQUES VILLENEUVE'S FATHER GILLES?

A) Japan

B) France

C) Canada

3 BAR USED TWO F1 TEST DRIVERS IN 2000. WHO WERE THEY?

A) Dick Dastardly and Muttley

B) Gary Neville and Graeme le Saux

C) Darren Manning and Patrick Lemarié

4 WHEN AND WHERE DID BAR SCORE ITS FIRST F1 POINTS?

A) Suzuka, Japan, 1999

B) Melbourne, Australia, 2000

C) Interlagos, Brazil, 2000

5 AT WHICH CIRCUIT DID JACQUES VILLENEUVE'S MOTORHOME GET STUCK IN A MUDDY CAR PARK IN 2000?

A) Silverstone

B) Hockenheim

C) The Nürburgring

RULES AND REGULATIONS

- Entrants must be 18 years of age or over.
- The competition is open to UK residents only.
- Only one entry per person is allowed.
- Entries from employees of Hazleton Publishing or British American Tobacco and their families are not permitted.
- The winning entrant will be notified by post. Information about the time and date of the prize will be made available as soon as possible.
- The draw will be made by an independent person.
- The winner's name and home town will be posted on the announcements page of our website: www.hazletonpublishing.com.
- A cash alternative is not an option.
- Entry to this competition is free apart from the postage stamp required to send your answers.
- No purchase is necessary.
- Hazleton Publishing, British American Racing and British American Tobacco do not take responsibility for entries lost, delayed or incomplete.

FOSTER'S BRITISH GRAND PRIX

DAVID COULTHARD SCORES A SECOND SUCCESSIVE HOME SUCCESS ON A BUSY SPORTING WEEKEND. WHILE HE WAS WINNING AN F1 RACE, SPECTATORS TRIED THEIR HAND AT RALLYCROSS IN THE CAR PARKS – OR RAN UP TO 10 MILES IN AN EFFORT TO REACH CHAOTIC SILVERSTONE

Armpit lane: McLaren's crew greets the winner (right) as he crosses the line on one of the few bits of road in Northamptonshire left navigable by the crap pre-race weather. Above, Coulthard salutes the lucky spectators who managed to overcome inept road traffic control and reach the circuit before the finish. Button lip: Britain's latest F1 hero did a passable impression of the retired Damon Hill by
a) monopolising the media attention and
b) finishing fifth

DAVID COULTHARD MIGHT BE LOGGED IN THE RECORD BOOKS AS OFFICIAL winner of the 2000 British Grand Prix, but in reality he was a distant third. The true Silverstone kings? Rain and mud were in a class of their own.

The Scot was as aware of that as anybody. During the deluge that was Friday afternoon, Coulthard came to a halt on the grass verge near Bridge Corner and waited for the tow truck to arrive. In a sequence pinched straight from Laurel and Hardy, the rescue vehicle arrived but became bogged down 20 yards before it reached the stricken McLaren. Shame it didn't happen elsewhere on the track. We could have talked about Keystone Copse...

The world watched as the track marshals resorted to a series of increasingly futile gestures – and secretly hoped a second truck might turn up and get stuck trying to get the first one out. The pragmatic Coulthard had a better idea: he took off his shoes and helped push his car out of the mire.

Never afraid to get his hands [or feet] dirty, Coulthard spoke like a true Scot: "I took my boots off because I pay for my shoes and the team pays for my socks. I prefer to ruin the socks." Never let it be said that he did not fully deserve to repeat the home victory he scored in 1999, if only for being one of the few blokes in the field who can not only string a sentence together, but can be dryly amusing with it.

The chaos lasted until raceday, when fog attempted to join rain and mud on the podium by blanketing the circuit and forcing postponement of vital helicopter traffic. As the fog's density remained constant, those in charge of the computer timing screens, with nothing better to do, broadcast the message: "The situation has just got worse. Ron Dennis is stuck in traffic."

The McLaren team boss fared worse than Mika Hakkinen when it came to getting into the circuit, which was surrounded by cars abandoned carelessly across the Northamptonshire countryside as frustrated ticket-holders gave up queuing and opted for shanks's pony. The Finn hitched a lift on the back of a motorcycle. Ironically, while thousands sat and seethed because they had been turned away from the tail-end of the jams, unable to make use of their £90 tickets, the race eventually went ahead in blazing sunshine.

Rubens Barrichello blasted into the lead from pole, but the Brazilian never looked comfortable and could not pull away from Heinz-Harald Frentzen's Jordan or Coulthard's McLaren. After the scheduled pit stops Coulthard was all over the Brazilian and passed him on lap 35, when a combination of wonky steering and hydraulic problems made Rubens easy prey shortly before the Ferrari number two spun out.

"After the good start this was the best chance of my life to win a race," Barrichello said. "Even though the car was offset I think I could have held off DC if it hadn't been for the hydraulics."

Coulthard, of course, wanted to hype up his overtaking manoeuvre as much as possible: "I remember Nigel Mansell's

THE CHAOS LASTED UNTIL RACEDAY, WHEN FOG BLANKETED THE CIRCUIT AND RON DENNIS GOT STUCK IN TRAFFIC

Sixth as a parrot: Frentzen (above) qualified and ran at the front, but was denied a decent finish when his Jordan's gearbox jammed in top and forced him to pit with only a few laps to go. Right, a very expensive pair of Schueys. Ralf leads Michael during their heated squabble in the early stages of the race

WEATHER RETORT

The most amusing thing about the mudbath that resulted from scheduling the British Grand Prix in April was watching Formula One's bigwigs stand up as one and claim that it was not their fault.

Working out that the weather might have caused problems in Britain at this time of year is hardly astrophysics. But Silverstone, it seemed, had moved from its traditional July date to Easter by osmosis.

Incoming BRDC president Jackie Stewart, clearly believing in a conspiracy, said: "This is not Silverstone's fault. The governing body chooses the dates. All major professional sporting events follow the sun – I don't care whether you are talking about the Masters, the Kentucky Derby, Ascot or the British Grand Prix."

Of course, FIA president Max Mosley insisted that the idea had been to follow the sun. "I'm sorry – but unfortunately we don't control the weather," Mosley said. "If the weather had been normal for April it wouldn't have happened. But there has been three times as much rain for April as usual. It is beyond our control."

In F1, surely nothing is beyond the control of ringmaster Bernie Ecclestone? "People are probably pointing the finger at me," he said. "I am sorry this race had to be scheduled at this time of the year, but it's not my doing. I get the blame for most things, but I don't deserve it for this. Internal politics caused the change of date. Besides, you can never predict the weather. It's England. I've been here in July when it's poured down. Silverstone has not taken the weather into consideration. They should have prayed."

One cynic suggested he might have meant "paid"...

THE BIGGEST CHEER OF THE AFTERNOON WAS SAVED FOR JENSON BUTTON, THE NEW HOME HERO

move on Nelson Piquet at Stowe in 1987," he said, "so I thought I'd give that a try. Thankfully it came off or I'd have looked like a complete idiot."

The Scotsman went on to win comfortably from Hakkinen, although he admitted having been prepared to cry in the car when he detected a small, but ultimately insignificant, gearbox problem in the dying laps.

The biggest cheer of the afternoon was reserved for the new home hero Jenson Button. The Englishman qualified sixth, ahead of team-mate Ralf Schumacher, and took his fairy-tale career to new heights by beating Michael Schumacher into the first corner. Fifth place was a relative anti-climax after that.

For Schumacher Snr, an eventual third was much better than he could have hoped for when he dropped to eighth at the start, after going onto the grass in a bid to find a way past everyone ahead. The grass? He should have consulted the bloke driving the tow truck... Michael said: "It was so wet that I found myself sitting there and going nowhere with the wheels spinning."

A subsequent battle between the two Schumachers included one hairy moment at Bridge, when Ralf gave big brother a chop, but the Ferrari eventually got past... only to get stuck behind Jacques Villeneuve's BAR. Ferrari's impeccable strategy meant he eventually snatched a podium from the jaws of obscurity, however.

Villeneuve was heading for sixth when his transmission failed four laps from home, letting Trulli claim the final point. Further rubbing salt into the Canadian's wounds, his motorhome crew later had trouble getting out of the circuit in his immaculate travelling palace. Nothing to do with the traffic, mind. It was stuck up to its axles in mud.

If ever Rubens Barrichello needed confirmation that this was not to be his season, Silverstone provided it.

Barrichello became the first man ever to take pole position while serving as Michael Schumacher's team-mate. His third F1 pole – all of them accomplished in wet-dry conditions – was nicked in the final seconds of qualifying on Silverstone's drying line.

Ferrari, of course, tried to get Schumacher to have the last flying lap of the session, but the German miscued his final warm-up lap and took the chequered flag a second too soon to begin a last-gasp flyer.

Staying in front was never going to be easy for Barrichello, whose steering wheel was aligned off-centre. The car understeered in one direction and oversteered in the other, which kept the field bunched up and enabled Schuey to stay in contention.

Barrichello survived until half-distance before a second hydraulics failure in four races caused him to spin off shortly after Coulthard had deprived him of the lead. In 1999, by contrast, his predecessor Eddie Irvine suffered only one mechanical failure in the whole season.

"I don't understand why it's been happening," Barrichello said. "Michael didn't have any problems and I'm disappointed that a couple of times I've had trouble when Ferrari has a record of being reliable."

The team's technical director Ross Brawn talked of a "statistical improbability" and sporting director Jean Todt said: "I think Rubens understands that the team is backing him and is giving him a good car." Is that the sound of maniacal, mildly Teutonic laughter we hear?

Full stop: the battling Zonta and de la Rosa [above left] and Barrichello [above] posted three of the race's five official retirements

STARTING GRID

Pos	Driver	Time
	4 Barrichello	1m25.703s
	5 Frentzen	1m25.706s
	1 Hakkinen	1m25.741s
	2 Coulthard	1m26.088s
	3 M Schumacher	1m26.161s
	10 Button	1m26.733s
	9 R Schumacher	1m26.786s
	19 Verstappen	1m26.793s
	7 Irvine	1m26.818s
	22 Villeneuve	1m27.025s
	6 Trulli	1m27.164s
	11 Fisichella	1m27.253s
	16 Diniz	1m27.301s
	8 Herbert	1m27.461s
	14 Alesi	1m27.559s
	23 Zonta	1m27.772s
	15 Heidfeld	1m27.806s
	17 Salo	1m28.110s
	18 de la Rosa	1m28.135s
	12 Wurz	1m28.205s
	20 Gené	1m28.253s
	21 Mazzacane	1m29.174s

April 23 2000
SILVERSTONE GRAND PRIX CIRCUIT, TOWCESTER, NORTHAMPTONSHIRE
CIRCUIT LENGTH: 3.194miles / 5.141km

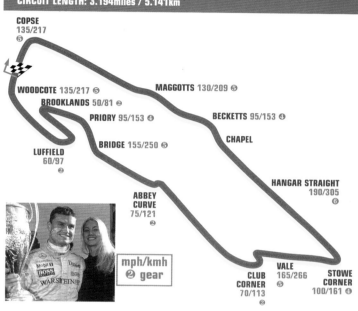

COPSE 135/217 ⑤
WOODCOTE 135/217 ⑤
MAGGOTTS 130/209 ⑤
BROOKLANDS 50/81 ②
PRIORY 95/153 ④
BECKETTS 95/153 ④
CHAPEL
BRIDGE 155/250 ⑤
LUFFIELD 60/97 ②
HANGAR STRAIGHT 190/305 ⑥
ABBEY CURVE 75/121 ②
VALE 165/266 ⑤
CLUB CORNER 70/113 ②
STOWE CORNER 100/161 ④

mph/kmh
❷ gear

RACE CLASSIFICATION

Pos	Driver	Nat	Car	Laps	Time
1	David Coulthard	GB	McLaren MP4/15-Mercedes V10	60	1h28m50.108s
2	Mika Hakkinen	FIN	McLaren MP4/15-Mercedes V10	60	+1.477s
3	Michael Schumacher	D	Ferrari F1 2000-Ferrari V10	60	+19.917s
4	Ralf Schumacher	D	Williams FW22-BMW V10	60	+41.312s
5	Jenson Button	GB	Williams FW22-BMW V10	60	+57.759s
6	Jarno Trulli	I	Jordan EJ10-Mugen V10	60	+1m19.273s
7	Giancarlo Fisichella	I	Benetton B200-Playlife V10		+1 lap
8	Mika Salo	FIN	Sauber C19-Petronas V10		+1 lap
9	Alexander Wurz	A	Benetton B200-Playlife V10		+1 lap
10	Jean Alesi	F	Prost AP03-Peugeot V10		+1 lap
11	Pedro Diniz	BR	Sauber C19-Petronas V10		+1 lap
12	Johnny Herbert	GB	Jaguar R1-Cosworth V10		+1 lap
13	Eddie Irvine	GB	Jaguar R1-Cosworth V10		+1 lap
14	Marc Gené	E	Minardi M02-Fondmetal V10		+1 lap
15	Gaston Mazzacane	RA	Minardi M02-Fondmetal V10		+1 lap
16	Jacques Villeneuve	CDN	BAR 002-Honda V10		+4 laps
17	Heinz-Harald Frentzen	D	Jordan EJ10-Mugen V10		+6 laps

Retirements	Nat	Car	Laps	Reason
Nick Heidfeld	D	Prost AP03-Peugeot V10	51	oil pressure
Ricardo Zonta	BR	BAR 002-Honda V10	36	spin
Rubens Barrichello	BR	Ferrari F1 2000-Ferrari V10	35	hydraulic pressure
Pedro de la Rosa	E	Arrows A21-Supertec V10	26	electronics
Jos Verstappen	NL	Arrows A21-Supertec V10	20	electrics

FASTEST LAP M Hakkinen 1m26.217s lap 56 (133.385mph/214.663kmh)

DRIVERS' CHAMPIONSHIP

1	Michael Schumacher	34
2	David Coulthard	14
3	Mika Hakkinen	12
4	Rubens Barrichello	9
	Ralf Schumacher	9
6	Giancarlo Fisichella	8
7	Jacques Villeneuve	5
8	Heinz-Harald Frentzen	4
	Jarno Trulli	4
10	Jenson Button	3
11	Mika Salo	1
	Ricardo Zonta	1

CONSTRUCTORS' CHAMPIONSHIP

1	Ferrari	43
2	McLaren-Mercedes	26
3	Williams-BMW	12
4	Benetton-Playlife	8
	Jordan-Mugen	8
6	BAR-Honda	6
7	Sauber-Petronas	1

HIS MASTER'S

VOICE

REUTERS

RTEL
NETWORKS

ITV'S ICONIC GUARDIAN OF THE MICROPHONE MURRAY WALKER WAS STALKING MOTOR SPORT COMMENTARY BOOTHS MORE THAN 30 YEARS BEFORE JENSON BUTTON LEARNED TO WALK. HE'S WATCHED – AND IN MANY CASES KNOWN – MOST OF THE RACING GREATS: JUAN MANUEL FANGIO; AYRTON SENNA; STIRLING MOSS; JIM CLARK; JACKIE STEWART; NIKI LAUDA; ALAIN PROST; JACK BRABHAM; A COUPLE OF HILLS; MICHAEL SCHUMACHER. YOU NAME THEM, HE'S REPORTED ON THEM IN SOME SHAPE OR FORM.

IN 1999, YOUNG BRITISH RACING HOPEFUL BUTTON HAD WATCHED THE BRITISH GP FROM THE SPECTATOR ENCLOSURE ALONGSIDE SILVERSTONE'S HANGAR STRAIGHT. IN 2000, HE HAD A SLIGHTLY BETTER VIEW – FROM A PRIVILEGED POSITION ON THE STARTING GRID, AT THE HELM OF A WILLIAMS-BMW.

SO WHAT DID ONE OF MOTOR RACING'S MOST SENIOR OBSERVERS MAKE OF THE MOST JUNIOR MEMBER OF THE F1 COMMUNITY?

MURRAY, YOU'VE SEEN A FEW PROMISING YOUNGSTERS IN YOUR TIME. WHAT WERE YOUR GENERAL IMPRESSIONS OF JENSON THIS SEASON?
"He has impressed me hugely – but the first thing I ought to say is that I have known the Button family for a long time. Back in the Seventies, when I was commentating almost every other weekend on rallycross events, usually at Lydden Hill, I used to watch his father, John, racing a VW Beetle. He was one of the quicker drivers, too, perhaps not absolutely the best but certainly always a force to be reckoned with. Jenson wasn't around at the time, of course, but I always remembered John as a very friendly guy."

WHEN DID YOU FIRST NOTICE BUTTON JNR MAKING AN IMPACT ON THE SPORT?
"I didn't know too much about Jenson's early career. I saw a few bits in the specialist press about how he was doing well in karting, but I first really cottoned on when he was racing successfully in Formula Ford. I might not have done, but F1 photographer Keith Sutton's agency was part-sponsoring him and kept bombarding me with pictures and press releases. That certainly brought him to my attention.

"JAPANESE FANS WENT FOR HIM IN A BIG WAY. THEY ARE USUALLY VERY CALM AND CONTROLLED, BUT THEY MOBBED HIM. WING MIRRORS WERE TORN OFF HIS ROAD CAR, THAT SORT OF THING"

"When he had the shoot-out against Bruno Junqueira to get the Williams drive earlier in the season I was delighted – and all the more so when he won. I've nothing at all against Junqueira, but I like to see young British guy coming through."

HE'S ATTRACTED SOME RAVE REVIEWS. WHAT DO YOU MAKE OF IT ALL?

"I have been overjoyed and amazed by how well he has gone. It only took him a couple of races to get some points – and with a bit of luck he could have scored on his debut. He has been a consistent top-six runner.

"His drive at Spa was incredible. It's a track where good drivers traditionally excel and to line up third there was fantastic. I thought he was superb at Suzuka, too. That's another place that sorts the men from the boys – yet he qualified and finished fifth and set fifth fastest race lap. He had no hope of beating the Ferraris or McLarens, but to win the second division battle with such conviction was marvellous."

HE'S HANDLED HIMSELF WELL ON THE TRACK. HAS HE ACQUITTED HIMSELF SO WELL OUT OF THE COCKPIT?

"I have been as impressed with him as a person as I have with his driving. I have been lucky enough to interview him a number of times him during the season and he is gigantically mature for someone of his age. He's very calm and has his feet on the ground, but he's no automaton – which you can't say about everyone in this business. He enjoys a laugh, gets on well with the media and lets his hair down when he's outside a racing environment. I find that quite endearing. All in all, I think he's a class act.

"It's not insignificant that the Japanese fans took to him in such a big way. As a nation, they are usually very calm and controlled – but they went crazy for Jenson in a similar way that they used to for Ayrton. It was almost hysterical idolatry. He and his dad got absolutely mobbed on their way in to the track each day. The wing mirrors were torn off their hire car, all that sort of stuff."

Idol hands: almost unknown before January 2000, Button was soon thrust into the limelight and became a popular target for fans [top]. At one point, Williams technical chief Patrick Head nicknamed him Hype Spice

Grin and bear it: Ralf Schumacher [above, right] got on well with his new partner, but didn't always see the funny side of being beaten. Top right, Jenson getting in and getting on with it in Monaco

DO YOU SEE ANYTHING OF A YOUNG SENNA OR SCHUMACHER IN THE WAY THE 2000-MODEL BUTTON PERFORMED?

"In the sense that he's supremely talented, yes, but I don't think his temperament is at all the same as the other two. He might well apply himself as thoroughly to the job as Schumacher does, but he's not quite so intense about it."

HE HAS HAD A FEW KNOCKERS IN THE PRESS. HAVE THE BRITISH TABLOIDS GIVEN HIM A FAIR DEAL?

"Newspapers have to be a fact of life for a young sportsman – and in Formula One they are looking for a new headline-maker to follow in the footsteps of Nigel Mansell and Damon Hill. As soon as this boy wonder arrived, it was obvious they would build him up. It's always the way, isn't it? They surround someone with adulation then, as soon as he falters, they go after him. They always try to cut down the tallest poppy. He had a bit of a slating at times, but by the end of the year they were fawning all over him again. And quite right, too."

YOU ARE OBVIOUSLY A FAN, BUT HAS HIS SUCCESS SURPRISED YOU AT ALL?

"Not really. He might have come directly from the British F3 series, which some people think is a big step up, but if you are good enough, like Ayrton Senna or Nelson Piquet were before him, it doesn't seem to be that difficult to adapt. And on the evidence of what we have seen so far, I think Jenson is exceptional."

DO YOU THINK WILLIAMS WAS WRONG TO LET HIM GO?

"In defence of Frank Williams, it's very easy for those who don't have to take such decisions to think he has made a mistake. At the time of the season when he had to make his choice, I don't think it was obvious that Jenson was as good as he has proved to be. But the next two seasons will do him good, learning about a new team environment with different people and a different engine. If things don't work out with Benetton and Renault, I'm sure there will always be future openings for him at Williams."

D'YOU THINK IT'S A PITY MORE TEAMS DON'T TAKE A CHANCE ON YOUNGSTERS IN THE WAY WILLIAMS DID THIS YEAR WITH JENSON?

"It is, but I can well understand why they don't. You have to be objective. This is a multi-million pound business and you need massive balls to invest in a new kid on the block in favour of an experienced, seasoned professional who will guarantee results. Look at McLaren and Mercedes. They have a fantastic support programme to help cultivate young drivers, but next year they are keeping Hakkinen and Coulthard for the sixth straight season.

"You have to give the Prost team a bit of credit for Jenson's emergence, because they had the foresight to test him in the first place, which is how Williams came to hear how good he was. It's a shame that it's so hard for young drivers to get the chance to make a name in F1, but I think Jenson has blazed a trail that might make it easier for them in future. It could take a while, mind you."

GRAN PREMIO MARLBORO DE ESPAÑA

FERRARI'S TEAM LEADER
PUTS ON HIS FINEST SCHOOL
BULLY IMPRESSION – BUT IT'S
NOT ENOUGH TO INTIMIDATE
THE DEFENDING CHAMP,
WHO NOTCHES HIS FIRST
WIN OF THE YEAR

Gain in Spain: Hakkinen (above) wrought misery
on Ferrari with an inch-perfect performance. Schuey
got some consolation, however, by getting his helmet
off in time for TV cameras to catch the post-race
perfection of his L'Oréal hairdo (right)

THERE WERE PLENTY OF PEOPLE READY TO TELL YOU exactly what they thought of Michael Schumacher after the Spanish Grand Prix.

Curiously, however, race winner Mika Hakkinen was not among them – despite his being victim of the Ferrari number one's peculiar starting technique, which could at best be described as "drunken".

The Finn had qualified on the front row, eight-hundredths of a second behind the German, and he was not the first driver this season [nor the last, come to that] to find his face full of weaving Ferrari when the start signal was given. But Hakkinen, beaming broadly after his first victory of the 2000 season let his arch-rival off the hook.

"My start wasn't fantastic," he said. "Michael moved and I was still sitting there. Then I realised he hadn't made a good getaway either. I went inside, realised he was closing the door and so switched to the outside, but the grip was low and I had to give up.

"My front wheel was almost level with his, so for him to push me onto the grass would have been dangerous and he wouldn't do that."

Of course he wouldn't, Mika. Never had a contentious moment in his life, that nice Herr Schumacher. Oddly, however, the two drivers who followed Hakkinen into the first corner – Schuey Jnr, up from fifth on the grid, and David Coulthard – both had contrary views to Hakkinen's by the close of play.

The German pulled away during the first few laps and it looked as though victory number four was his for the taking, but Hakkinen was back with him by the time the first scheduled pit stops came around.

FERRARI'S CREW GAVE SCHUEY A PREMATURE SIGNAL TO REJOIN THE RACE, BUT CHIEF MECHANIC NIGEL STEPNEY WAS STILL ATTACHED TO THE CAR VIA HIS REFUELLING HOSE

Then it all started to go wrong for people wearing red trousers. Ferrari's crew gave Schuey a premature signal to rejoin the race, but chief mechanic Nigel Stepney was still attached to the car via his refuelling hose. As the German engaged the clutch and sped away, he was left to wonder who had installed sleeping policemen in the pit lane since the start of the race. His right rear wheel clobbered Englishman Stepney, who was fortunate to escape with nothing worse than painful ankle ligament damage.

It was the third race in a row that Schumacher had driven into someone. He hit his jackman in Imola, a photographer at Silverstone and now his chief mechanic. Some hat trick.

Schumacher said: "I felt I was driving over something, looked in the mirror and saw one mechanic down. I asked the team over the radio what was going on but obviously they were checking him out so they didn't respond."

At this point Ferrari had about 90 seconds in which to find someone fit who could give the incoming Rubens Barrichello a tank of unleaded. Up stepped Andrea Vaccari, who performed admirably and even got the Brazilian back on track in fourth

Art attack: is there any meritocratic reason for using a shot of Jean Alesi [above]? No, frankly, but it's a lovely picture and the art editor sulks if we don't allow his heart to rule his head. This is balanced, however, by a snap of Pedro de la Rosa leading a bunch of midfield dullards [right]

SCOTSMAN THE BRAVE

There can have been few braver or more impressive Formula One performances than David Coulthard's second place in Barcelona.

It is not often that any sportsman has to cope with a near-death experience and fierce competition in the space of a couple of days, but Coulthard travelled to Spain within hours of having survived an aeroplane crash in France. He, fiancée Heidi and trainer Andy escaped with minor injuries. Their two charter pilots perished.

The Scot was given a weekend off press duties and managed to skirt around telling anyone that he was suffering from three cracked ribs. In the circumstances, his performance was sensational.

McLaren team boss Ron Dennis said: "David's reaction has been quite remarkable – dignified, professional and compassionate. Above all else he has found a way to do the job, and he has grown stronger for this experience."

Coulthard [with, from left above, Heidi, Merc big cheese Jürgen Hubbert and Ron Dennis] didn't spray champagne on the podium, as a mark of respect to those who died, and was adamant that nothing had changed his resolve.

Coulthard said: "The experience has given me a slightly different perspective on life. I'm determined not to give up or give way in my battle to win grands prix. That's why I'm taking every inch I can on the track. That's the way it's going to be all year. No one's going to get any favours from me."

As he spoke, post-race, however, he couldn't help but wince a little. "The irony," he said, "is that Heidi and Andy are getting better every day, but I've been getting worse because I've been pounding around in the car."

Unlucky strike: BARbecue time for Villeneuve after his Honda V10 gets hotter under the collar than Coulthard did about Schuey's defence

HE WAITED UNTIL I HAD COMMITTED AND IT WAS VERY, VERY CLOSE TO BEING A BIG SHUNT

DAVID COULTHARD ON MICHAEL SCHUMACHER'S BLOCKING TACTICS

place, ahead of Coulthard. Vaccari didn't do as well 20 laps later when Schumacher came in for his second stop, at the same time as Hakkinen, because a fuel rig problem cost the German 10 seconds. Game, set and match, Finland.

Coulthard got his revenge at the second set of stops, too, because he vaulted past Ralf and Barrichello to take third. Worse still for Ferrari, it was soon clear that Schumacher had a tyre problem, because his car was all over the road even without Hakkinen being there for him to weave at.

On lap 47 Coulthard made a pitch for second place at the end of the straight. Very, very late, Schumacher moved across. The Scot got past cleanly on the next lap, but was less than impressed with the abruptness of Schuey's initial defence.

He said: "I don't think it was at all fair. He waited until I had committed and it was very, very close to being a big shunt. Some die-hards will tell me not to be a pansy, but we were both on the limit and when you're going at that speed, you have to trust the guys around you."

Schumacher mumbled something about rules being rules and said: "If you don't do it, you look stupid." Now armed only with a limping Ferrari, he went on to defend himself against his next would-be assailant, baby brother Ralf [see sidebar].

It was a typical day in his life. Too quick out of the pits, too aggressive with his manoeuvres, too many stops, two new enemies and only two world championship points.

Too bad.

BROTHERS AT ARMS

There was a time when Ralf Schumacher [with a close relative, left] would obediently sidestep to make room for anything red that was driven by his brother, but no more. At Silverstone two weeks previously, Ralf had held Michael up during the early laps of the race, which almost caused an incident at Bridge corner. [You can just see it back home in Kerpen, can't you? "Mummy, mummy. Michael has just put me in the gravel at 160mph. Can it be my turn to watch some rubbish American TV cop show dubbed into German? Please? Please?"]

In Spain Schuey Jnr spotted another chance to stake a claim to sit in the front of the car with dad next time they went out for a family picnic. With 15 laps to go the Williams-BMW driver was gaining on his brother and had designs on bagging another third place.

Michael had a tyre problem, and was on his way into the pits, yet he obstructed his sibling for a full lap and the two eventually brushed wheels, which let the chasing Rubens Barrichello slip neatly into third. Cue much discontent.

"Mummy..."

Although he attempted not to be too outspoken in public, Ralf was seething. "What Michael did was absolutely senseless," he said, before stomping off to squabble with his brother in a motorhome, away from prying eyes.

Michael said: "I can't help it if he is angry with me. Racing is racing and I'm not giving anyone any favours, including my brother. If he doesn't understand that, it's hard luck. In Silverstone he purposely didn't give me space, so he has no reason to complain.

"I touched him on the sidepod, but there was nothing I could do. He was pushing me and I wanted to defend my line. I couldn't do much about it because I had a puncture and my car understeered a lot when I turned into the corner."

The wounds did not last. Two weeks later the pair were putting on their customarily harmonious front and denied any sort of argument had even taken place. It was an admirable attempt at unity marred only by one minor detail: they were talking bollocks.

STARTING GRID

3 M Schumacher 1m20.974s

1 Hakkinen 1m21.052s

4 Barrichello 1m21.416s

2 Coulthard 1m21.422s

9 R Schumacher 1m21.605s

22 Villeneuve 1m21.963s

6 Trulli 1m22.006s

5 Frentzen 1m22.135s

7 Irvine 1m 22.370s

10 Button 1m22.385s

19 Verstappen 1m 22.421s

17 Salo 1m22.443s

11 Fisichella 1m22.569s

8 Herbert 1m22.781s

16 Diniz 1m22.841s

23 Zonta 1m22.882s

14 Alesi 1m22.894s

12 Wurz 1m23.010s

15 Heidfeld 1m23.033s

20 Gené 1m23.486s

21 Mazzacane 1m24.257s

* qualified 9th fastest, but started at the back of the grid due to fuel irregularities

18 de la Rosa *

May 7 2000
CIRCUIT DE CATALUNYA, MONTMELO, BARCELONA
CIRCUIT LENGTH: 2.939mles / 4.730km

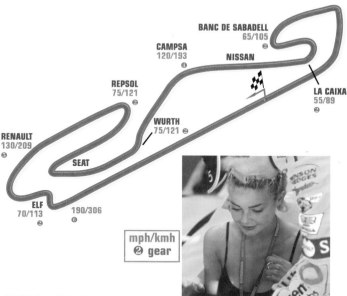

BANC DE SABADELL 65/105

CAMPSA 120/193

NISSAN

REPSOL 75/121

LA CAIXA 55/89

WURTH 75/121

RENAULT 130/209

SEAT

ELF 70/113

190/306

mph/kmh
❷ gear

RACE CLASSIFICATION

Pos	Driver	Nat	Car	Laps	Time
1	Mika Hakkinen	FIN	McLaren MP4-15-Mercedes V10	65	1h33m55.390s
2	David Coulthard	GB	McLaren MP4-15-Mercedes V10	65	+16.066s
3	Rubens Barrichello	BR	Ferrari F1 2000-Ferrari V10	65	+29.112s
4	Ralf Schumacher	D	Williams FW22-BMW V10	65	+37.311s
5	Michael Schumacher	D	Ferrari F1 2000-Ferrari V10	65	+47.983s
6	Heinz-Harald Frentzen	D	Jordan EJ10-Mugen V10	65	+1m21.925s
7	Mika Salo	FIN	Sauber C19-Petronas V10		+1 lap
8	Ricardo Zonta	BR	BAR 002-Honda V10		+1 lap
9	Giancarlo Fisichella	I	Benetton B200-Playlife V10		+1 lap
10	Alexander Wurz	A	Benetton B200-Playlife V10		+1 lap
11	Eddie Irvine	GB	Jaguar R1-Cosworth V10		+1 lap
12	Jarno Trulli	I	Jordan EJ10-Mugen V10		+1 lap
13	Johnny Herbert	GB	Jaguar R1-Cosworth V10		+1 lap
14	Marc Gené	E	Minardi M02-Fondmetal V10		+2 laps
15	Gaston Mazzacane	RA	Minardi M02-Fondmetal V10		+2 laps
16	Nick Heidfeld	D	Prost AP03-Peugeot V10		+3 laps
17	Jenson Button	GB	Williams FW22-BMW V10		+4 laps
Retirements		**Nat**	**Car**	**Laps**	**Reason**
Jos Verstappen		NL	Arrows A21-Supertec V10	25	gearbox
Jacques Villeneuve		CDN	BAR 002-Honda V10	21	oil pressure/engine
Jean Alesi		F	Prost AP03-Peugeot V10	1	accident
Pedro de la Rosa		E	Arrows A21-Supertec V10	1	accident
Pedro Diniz		BR	Sauber C19-Petronas V10	0	spin

FASTEST LAP M Hakkinen 1m24.470s lap 28 (125.260mph/201.586kmh)

DRIVERS' CHAMPIONSHIP

1	Michael Schumacher	36
2	Mika Hakkinen	22
3	David Coulthard	20
4	Rubens Barrichello	13
5	Ralf Schumacher	12
6	Giancarlo Fisichella	8
7	Heinz-Harald Frentzen	5
	Jacques Villeneuve	5
9	Jarno Trulli	4
10	Jenson Button	3
11	Mika Salo	1
	Ricardo Zonta	1

CONSTRUCTORS' CHAMPIONSHIP

1	Ferrari	49
2	McLaren-Mercedes	42
3	Williams-BMW	15
4	Jordan-Mugen	9
5	Benetton-Playlife	8
6	BAR-Honda	6
7	Sauber-Petronas	1

WARSTEINER GRAND PRIX OF EUROPE

GERMAN F1 FANS USUALLY
HAVE A LITTLE BLOOD IN THEIR
LAGERSTREAM. THIS TIME THEY
HAD A SPLASH OF RAINWATER, TOO,
BUT ANOTHER SCHUEY WIN TOOK THEIR
MIND OFF THE WEATHER AND ALLOWED
THEM TO FOCUS ON THE WEEKEND'S
MAIN BUSINESS – DRINKING

Victor's gauntlet: Ferrari's number one raises his arm in triumph [left] after scoring his first win on home soil for the Prancing Horse. So happy did it make him that he even pretended to be best of mates with those two pesky blokes in grey overalls who sometimes give him a hard time

MUCH OF THE FUSS SURROUNDING DAVID COULTHARD'S PLANE CRASH HAD subsided by the time Formula One decamped to Germany for the Grand Prix of Europe, so there wasn't quite such a media scrum when he bagged his first pole position for more than 30 races.

It was one hell of an achievement – and not the sort of thing you expect from someone nursing broken ribs. But driving a racing car, Coulthard pointed out, was not the sort of thing such injuries prevented. In fact he went into considerable detail on the subject – in a room packed with about 500 journalists.

"I have sore ribs and my fiancée Heidi has a sore chest, so everything's a bit difficult," the Scot said. "I haven't had sex for more than two weeks and the dog has been looking a bit nervous."

At this point Michael Schumacher, sitting alongside, made as if to edge away, but Coulthard was as quick as he had been during the one-hour qualifying session just gone. "Sorry," he said to the German, "but I don't find you attractive."

The only bleak note about pole position was that it had become something of an albatross. Not for 11 races – when Mika Hakkinen won in Hungary the previous season – had the fastest qualifier gone on to win a grand prix. "It's a bizarre statistic," Coulthard said.

Not as bizarre, however, as his tardy start. Once almost unbeatable off the line, the Scotsman was still gazing at the start lights when Schumacher and Hakkinen zipped past.

The Finn made an electrifying getaway, which he described as "very, very close to perfect", and stormed through a gap between Coulthard and Schumacher to lead into the first corner. Schumacher, predictably, did not yield easily. "As Mika moved sharply right I was surprised," Michael said, "and there was nowhere I could go so we touched – his right rear to my left front. It was probably unnecessary and I think he knows that."

Possibly unnecessary to mention it, too, Michael, as it didn't do you any harm.

While the top two were unscathed after their brush, sixth-fastest qualifier Jarno Trulli was put straight out of the race when fellow Italian Giancarlo Fisichella clipped his Jordan's rear wheel. The Benetton plugged on unaffected... at least until a private test in Valencia, Spain, the following week, when he did the same thing to the same driver and launched himself 20 feet into the air.

They are still friends, however, and Fisichella is unable to slag Trulli off in front of English reporters because the only words he feels comfortable with are "very", "pleased" and "happy".

Back in the race, Schumacher pressed Hakkinen until the 11th lap, when he sneaked past as the first signs of rain appeared. Unlike Schuey, Hakkinen is not renowned for his ability in the wet, but the pass – when it came – was a complete gift. "I knew

THE FINN MADE AN ELECTRIFYING GETAWAY AND STORMED THROUGH A GAP BETWEEN COULTHARD AND SCHUMACHER TO LEAD INTO THE FIRST CORNER

Ale storm: The Schuey faithful concentrate hard on trying to stand up straight as their marathon drinking session reaches its climax. Above, Hakkinen started the race faster than the average German F1 fan polishes off a stein, but he had no answer to "the Michael" (as he likes to call him) once it started raining

SCRAP MERCHANTS

There's nothing like a healthy bust-up between F1 drivers to smooth the show along. This time it was the turn of Jordan's Heinz-Harald Frentzen and Arrows's Jos Verstappen [right and left respectively, above] to choose handbags at 20 paces.

The problem? Qualifying. The German was on a flying [relatively speaking] lap when he came up behind Verstappen, who had not long since left the pits. Initially the Dutchman blocked the advancing Jordan, then – once Frentzen's hot lap was screwed – he let it past before moving ahead again as the riled Teuton slowed up to remonstrate. Much shaking of fists and long, complicated swear words later, the pair returned to the pits.

Frentzen said: "Someone did not bother looking in his mirror and it destroyed my chances of a good lap. I don't want to name names, but Verstappen is a fool."

He confronted the object of his ire before the race, but the Arrows driver pleaded puzzlement. Verstappen said: "I simply didn't see him, but I told him if he reacts like that again I will have him off."

Quite what Frentzen did to upset Verstappen in the first few hundred metres is unclear, but the Dutchman was true to his word. At the first corner the Jordan driver had to veer off onto the grass to avoid some fool [© H-H Frentzen], but it was hardly worth taking avoiding action because his Mugen Honda V10 blew within two laps.

Verstappen carried on in combative mood by racing hard with Eddie Irvine's Jaguar, until they clashed and caused the following Ralf Schumacher to pile into them. Irvine continued for another few corners until his rear wing broke away and caused him to spin off for good. Verstappen made it a little further before he, too, went off the road. He described it as a "spin"; those who saw him clambering from the steaming wreck regarded it as a substantial accident.

BARRICHELLO WAS THE ONLY MAN IN THE RACE WHO ATTEMPTED – AT HIS TEAM'S BEHEST – TO GET AWAY WITH A THREE-STOP STRATEGY

the chicane was only place he could overtake," Hakkinen said. "But I was cautious and lifted because I didn't want to throw it away. But I hope it doesn't happen any more." [Moral of the tale: don't bloody lift off if there's a rampaging German breathing down your neck.]

The Ferrari star promptly eased away into the distance and stayed ahead when the top two stopped for wet tyres four laps later. To his credit, Hakkinen never lost touch with Schumacher for the remainder of the race, although he complained about slower cars failing to observe blue warning flags as he came up to lap them later on. Perhaps he was just bitter because he had earlier slowed up without marshals having advised him to do so.

"It's one of the best days of my life," Schumacher said, "to record my first victory with Ferrari in front of a German crowd. The guys came here with all this bad weather, so I hope I warmed up their hearts a bit." [Warming their hearts is all very well, Michael, but you'd do better to persuade them to kick the mullet hairdos and fluorescent turquoise shellsuits that are all the rage in the Eifel mountains.]

It wasn't quite such a cheerful day for Schuey's team-mate Rubens Barrichello. After he lost 15 seconds queuing behind Schumacher for wet tyres during a comedy Ferrari pit stop, the Brazilian was the only man in the race who attempted – at his team's behest – to get away with a three-stop strategy. This condemned him to spend the afternoon in a] traffic and b] heavy spray, which left him to finish fourth behind Coulthard. Later, he described the strategy as "a disaster", although Ferrari's master tactician Ross Brawn didn't agree.

"He'll probably see it differently when he's cooled down," Brawn said. "We asked him to overtake a lot of cars, but he's a racing driver – that's what he's supposed to do."

For three years Nick Heidfeld had known nothing but success. As a McLaren-Mercedes junior he had wrapped up the German Formula Three title before going on to win a record-equalling number of races on his way to securing the FIA F3000 Championship – the approved F1 feeder series.

But then he joined Prost.

After a dodgy start to the season [when his car seldom ran for more than five minutes at a time] the Nürburgring, his first grand prix on home soil, promised a change of fortune – particularly when he qualified 13th, half a second clear of team-mate Jean Alesi.

Heidfeld hung on to his precious result for at least 30 of the 1440 minutes that that remained before kick-off – because that's when the scrutineers discovered that his chassis, which hitherto had all the finesse of a darts player in a ballet skirt – was in fact 2kg underweight. And the penalty was certain disqualification. So that'll be no home grand prix, then.

Team boss Alain Prost said: "We had some new parts with us, but when we put them on Nick's car for the first time we unfortunately made a mistake in calculating the car weight."

As he wandered glumly away from the circuit, Heidfeld said: "I have mixed feelings – but the bad ones are stronger."

Duel carriageway: Irvine battles in vain with the sparkling de la Rosa (above left), who gave Arrows its first point of the season. Above, Heidfeld was looking forward to showing what he could do on home soil. He spectated most impressively, apparently

STARTING GRID

2 Coulthard
1m17.529s

3 M Schumacher
1m17.667s

1 Hakkinen
1m17.785s

4 Barrichello
1m18.227s

9 R Schumacher
1m18.515s

6 Trulli
1m18.612s

11 Fisichella
1m18.697s

7 Irvine
1m18.703s

22 Villeneuve
1m18.742s

5 Frentzen
1m18.830s

10 Button
1m18.887s

18 de la Rosa
1m19.024s

19 Verstappen
1m19.190s

12 Wurz
1m19.378s

16 Diniz
1m19.422s

8 Herbert
1m19.638s

14 Alesi
1m19.651s

23 Zonta
1m19.766s

17 Salo
1m19.814s

20 Gené
1m20.162s

21 Mazzacane
1m21.015s

15 N Heidfeld D Prost AP03-Peugeot V10 qualified 13th (1m19.147s) but was excluded from the race because his car was under the legal weight limit

May 21 2000
NÜRBURGRING, NÜRBURG/EIFEL, GERMANY
CIRCUIT LENGTH: 2.831miles / 4.556km

mph/kmh
② gear

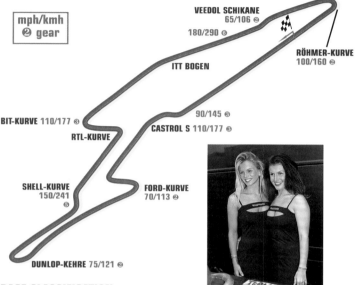

VEEDOL SCHIKANE 65/106 ②
180/290 ⑥
RÖHMER-KURVE 100/160 ②
ITT BOGEN
90/145 ③
BIT-KURVE 110/177 ③
CASTROL S 110/177 ③
RTL-KURVE
SHELL-KURVE 150/241 ⑤
FORD-KURVE 70/113 ②
DUNLOP-KEHRE 75/121 ②

RACE CLASSIFICATION

Pos	Driver	Nat	Car	Laps	Time
1	Michael Schumacher	D	Ferrari F1 2000-Ferrari V10	67	1h42m00.307s
2	Mika Hakkinen	FIN	McLaren MP4-15-Mercedes V10	67	+13.821s
3	David Coulthard	GB	McLaren MP4-15-Mercedes V10		+1 lap
4	Rubens Barrichello	BR	Ferrari F1 2000-Ferrari V10		+1 lap
5	Giancarlo Fisichella	I	Benetton B200-Playlife V10		+1 lap
6	Pedro de la Rosa	E	Arrows A21-Supertec V10		+1 lap
7	Pedro Diniz	BR	Sauber C19-Petronas V10		+2 laps
8	Gaston Mazzacane	RA	Minardi M02-Fondmetal V10		+2 laps
9	Jean Alesi	F	Prost AP03-Peugeot V10		+2 laps
10	Jenson Button	GB	Williams FW22-BMW V10		+5 laps
11	Johnny Herbert	GB	Jaguar R1-Cosworth V10		+6 laps
12	Alexander Wurz	A	Benetton B200-Playlife V10		+6 laps

Retirements	Nat	Car	Laps	Reason
Ricardo Zonta	BR	BAR 002-Honda V10	51	gearbox/spin
Marc Gené	E	Minardi M02-Fondmetal V10	47	throttle
Jacques Villeneuve	CDN	BAR 002-Honda V10	46	engine valve
Eddie Irvine	GB	Jaguar R1-Cosworth V10	29	accident/rear wing
Jos Verstappen	NL	Arrows A21-Supertec V10	29	accident
Ralf Schumacher	D	Williams FW22-BMW V10	29	accident
Mika Salo	FIN	Sauber C19-Petronas V10	27	driveshaft/spin
Heinz-Harald Frentzen	D	Jordan EJ10-Mugen V10	2	engine
Jarno Trulli	I	Jordan EJ10-Mugen V10	0	accident

FASTEST LAP M Schumacher 1m22.269s lap 8 (123.880mph/199.365kmh)

DRIVERS' CHAMPIONSHIP

1	Michael Schumacher	46
2	Mika Hakkinen	28
3	David Coulthard	24
4	Rubens Barrichello	16
5	Ralf Schumacher	12
6	Giancarlo Fisichella	10
7	Heinz-Harald Frentzen	5
	Jacques Villeneuve	5
9	Jarno Trulli	4
10	Jenson Button	3
11	Pedro de la Rosa	1
	Mika Salo	1
	Ricardo Zonta	1

CONSTRUCTORS' CHAMPIONSHIP

1	Ferrari	62
2	McLaren-Mercedes	52
3	Williams-BMW	15
4	Benetton-Playlife	10
5	Jordan-Mugen	9
6	BAR-Honda	6
7	Arrows-Supertec	1
	Sauber-Petronas	1

GRAND PRIX DE MONACO

MONEY, GLAMOUR, PRESTIGE AND OLD LADIES TAKING POODLES FOR A CARRY AROUND THE BLOCK – IT'S EASY TO SEE WHY MONTE CARLO HAS SUCH KUDOS. FIVE MINUTES DOWN THE ROAD FROM HIS APARTMENT, DAVID COULTHARD SAVOURS HIS SECOND WIN OF THE YEAR

Spray rise: Coulthard (above) celebrates being the first Scot to win the Monaco GP since he was two years old. Left, given that they earn almost as much per season as Chelsea spend on footballers in a week, you'd think they'd at least be able to start a race without problems. Schuey leads away — and it took only three attempts to get started

HE MIGHT HAVE BEEN HELPED A LITTLE BY OTHERS' MISFORTUNES, BUT DAVID Coulthard felt not the slightest bit guilty after becoming the first Brit to win the Monaco Grand Prix since Jackie Stewart in 1973.

In the early stages of the race he looked set for a frustrating afternoon, gummed behind Jarno Trulli's Jordan while Michael Schumacher cruised towards what appeared to be an inevitable fourth victory of the season.

When those two obstacles vanished for technical reasons, however, the Scot was not about to shed any tears. Overtaking in the principality is nigh on impossible, unless you are riding a scooter through one of the traffic jams that proliferate at grand prix time, and he was happy to profit whatever the circumstances.

"I accept that I benefited from the other guys' problems," Coulthard said, his overalls drenched in a peculiar cocktail of sweat and champagne, "but that is Monaco. I have had my own fair share of bad luck here over the years so I'm more than happy to take this win."

Success completed a collection of victory stamps that Coulthard particularly cherishes. He said: "There have always been certain races I wanted to win. Spa, because it is my favourite track. The British Grand Prix, because it is my home race. Monza, because there is nothing quite like an Italian crowd for F1. And Monaco, because technically this is one of the most difficult and challenging tracks for any driver."

It took three attempts to get the race started. The first was aborted because Alexander Wurz stalled his Benetton on the grid and caused a minor delay. Then a "computer fault" [© the FIA] caused the start lights to malfunction, although the field steamed away nonetheless. Some cynics suggested this neatly covered the fact that Michael Schumacher might have rocketed away too soon from pole position, but the legitimacy of his start soon became immaterial. Before drivers had chance to register that they were going to have to do it all again, Monaco virgin Jenson Button rammed Pedro de la Rosa at the Grand Hotel hairpin [formerly Loews] and provoked a snarl-up that blocked the track [see sidebar].

TRULLI MANAGED TO FRUSTRATE COULTHARD FOR 37 LAPS UNTIL HIS JORDAN'S GEARBOX GAVE WAY, WHICH PROMPTED A JUSTIFIABLE POST-RACE SULK

The third and final start followed the expected script, because Schumacher easily beat fellow front-row qualifier Trulli into the first corner before disappearing over the horizon. The Italian subsequently managed to frustrate Coulthard for 37 laps until his Jordan's gearbox gave way, which prompted a justifiable post-race sulk.

By that time, Schumacher's lead was more than half a minute and he could afford to breeze home. His only scheduled pit stop was slick and the outcome looked settled until lap 56, when the German's rear suspension broke. The official Ferrari excuse was that the defective part had been burnt through by exhaust heat, although rivals claimed they had seen Schumacher have at least one brush with the barriers.

Behind Coulthard, Heinz-Harald Frentzen looked sure to take

Trulli deeply maddening: the winner grits his teeth [above] as he experiences a sensation familiar to all Brits who become entrapped behind caravan-towing Dutchmen in the Lake District during July and August. Trulli's stout defence allowed Schuey [right] to open up a gargantuan lead before his normally bullet-proof car fell to bits

SLOGANS RUN

If there is one place you do not want to break down in Monte Carlo, it is the section between the Grand Hotel hairpin and the tunnel entrance. If you want to get back to the pits for your spare car, it involves a convoluted one-mile run.

That does not sound a lot for blokes who are well paid to be among the world's fittest athletes, but even Michael Johnson might find running a bit of a challenge if he was wearing a thick, quilted, sponsorship-infested suit and a crash helmet. During the course of the weekend, several drivers were forced to tackle this arduous, up-and-down assault course.

Jacques Villeneuve set the trend. The Canadian ventured out early in qualifying to take advantage of the empty track, but a traffic-free circuit has no benefit when your engine blows up after half a lap. With no other cars on the track, the TV producer focused for almost 10 minutes on the jogging Villeneuve as he made his way through the tunnel, down past the chicane, alongside the harbour, past Tabac and, finally, into the British American Racing pit to collect his T-car. Race day provided an ever better spectacle – and a contest much closer than anything we saw on track. When Pedro de la Rosa and Jenson Button clashed at the Grand Hotel hairpin on lap one, they brought several other cars to a standstill and blocked the track [above]. Button, de la Rosa, Ricardo Zonta, Pedro Diniz, Marc Gené and Nick Heidfeld were all involved in a mini-marathon in a bid to get back for the restart. Villeneuve was also involved in the tangle, but stayed calmly in his car, waited for the blockage to be cleared and drove back to the pits. He had been there, seen it and run it – and wasn't about to go through it again.

FISICHELLA – WHO USUALLY THRIVES ON THE STREETS OF MONTE CARLO – SLITHERED UP THE ORDER AS OTHERS DROPPED OUT

second until he clobbered the barriers shortly before the end, so Rubens Barrichello salvaged minor consolation for Ferrari after a steady run from the lower reaches of the top 10. Giancarlo Fisichella – who usually thrives on the streets of Monte Carlo – also slithered up the order as others dropped out. The Italian gave his out-of-sorts team a boost by taking third.

If these two were surprised about the fruitfulness of their afternoon, it hardly matched the delight at hitherto unreliable Jaguar, which scored its first-ever world championship points after Eddie Irvine finished fourth.

The Ulsterman described it as "one of the hardest races of my life" after having to contend with a badly blistered foot and a broken drinks bottle.

Throughout the weekend, Mika Hakkinen had just reason to feel that someone was conspiring against him. Every time the Finn attempted a qualifying lap, one of his rivals would fly off the circuit in front of him and hold him up. Perhaps there were good odds available on Schumacher in Spain, because Pedro de la Rosa and Marc Gené were among the offenders.

Things barely improved in the race. After spending the early laps stuck behind Frentzen's Jordan, a loose bit of McLaren started rattling around the cockpit and eventually wedged itself behind the brake pedal. It took a 60-second pit stop to have the offending part removed.

Hakkinen battled back from 14th to sixth before gearbox trouble slowed him up. He spent the final stages of the race bottled up behind the Sauber of his compatriot and namesake Salo.

But if the defending champ felt hard done by, Jean Alesi's plight was worse. The Franco-Sicilian lined up an improbable seventh in his canine-mannered Prost, but dropped out when his transmission packed up.

As always, he was the epitome of restraint: "Give me a few bits of wool to stick on the car, a good gust of Mistral wind and I could come up with a better aerodynamic package on the bridge at Avignon than the team has managed in the wind tunnel."

Monaco's first corner, Ste Dévote, is traditionally an accident blackspot...

Often, it's the scene of a disruptive first-lap pile-up – but this year it was a source of calamity throughout the race.

The worst affected was Ralf Schumacher, who hit the barriers hard and ended up with a three-inch cut in his leg. Although the injury was promptly stitched up, it did briefly threaten his participation in the following Canadian GP.

Every so often, the cameras would pan to a stricken car in the wall at – or close to – Ste Dévote. Schuey Jnr apart, Pedro Diniz, Gaston Mazzacane, Heinz-Harald Frentzen, Ricardo Zonta and Alexander Wurz all came to grief...

Zonta blamed the surface. "It was very slippery if you got on the middle of the track," he said. "I hit a bump that sent me off line and into the wall."

Eddie Jordan received an apology from Frentzen and accepted it graciously – even though it cost his team a certain second place. "We all make mistakes," the Irishman said. But Benetton team manager Flavio Briatore was less sympathetic about Wurz's plight. "Anyone watching TV could see how good he is," he said.

In the misadventure stakes, however, no contemporary F1 racer came close to matching Seventies grand prix driver Alex Ribeiro. Nowadays employed to chauffeur the official F1 medical car around the track, he crashed it heavily at Tabac corner on Saturday morning.

Great barrier grief: Ralf Schumacher freed himself from his trashed Williams [above]... then noticed a nasty gash in his leg. He wasn't the only one who made a porridge of Ste Dévote. Above left, Fisichella didn't shine as much as he normally does in Monte Carlo, but others' carelessness gifted him a podium

STARTING GRID

3 M Schumacher 1m19.475s

6 Trulli 1m19.746s

2 Coulthard 1m19.888s

5 Frentzen 1m19.961s

1 Hakkinen 1m20.241s

4 Barrichello 1m20.416s

14 Alesi 1m20.494s

11 Fisichella 1m20.703s

9 R Schumacher 1m20.742s

7 Irvine 1m20.743s

8 Herbert 1m20.792s

12 Wurz 1m20.871s

17 Salo 1m21.561s

10 Button 1m21.605s

19 Verstappen 1m21.738s

18 de la Rosa 1m21.832s

22 Villeneuve 1m21.848s

15 Heidfeld 1m22.017s

16 Diniz 1m22.136s

23 Zonta 1m22.324s

20 Gené 1m23.721s

21 Mazzacane 1m23.794s

June 4 2000
MONTE CARLO STREET CIRCUIT
CIRCUIT LENGTH: 2.094miles / 3.370km

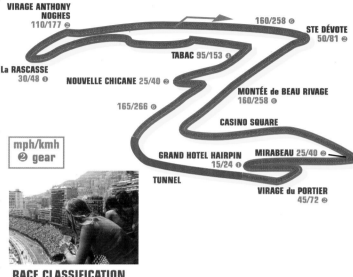

VIRAGE ANTHONY NOGHES 110/177 ❷

160/258 ❻

STE DÉVOTE 50/81 ❷

TABAC 95/153 ❹

La RASCASSE 30/48 ❶

NOUVELLE CHICANE 25/40 ❷

MONTÉE de BEAU RIVAGE 160/258 ❻

165/266 ❻

CASINO SQUARE

mph/kmh ❷ gear

GRAND HOTEL HAIRPIN 15/24 ❶

MIRABEAU 25/40 ❷

TUNNEL

VIRAGE du PORTIER 45/72 ❷

RACE CLASSIFICATION

Pos	Driver	Nat	Car	Laps	Time
1	David Coulthard	GB	McLaren MP4-15-Mercedes V10	78	1h49m28.213s
2	Rubens Barrichello	BR	Ferrari F1 2000-Ferrari V10	78	+15.889s
3	Giancarlo Fisichella	I	Benetton B200-Playlife V10	78	+18.522s
4	Eddie Irvine	GB	Jaguar R1-Cosworth V10	78	+1m05.924s
5	Mika Salo	FIN	Sauber C19-Petronas V10	78	+1m20.774s
6	Mika Hakkinen	FIN	McLaren MP4-15-Mercedes V10		+1 lap
7	Jacques Villeneuve	CDN	BAR 002-Honda V10		+1 lap
8	Nick Heidfeld	D	Prost AP03-Peugeot V10		+1 lap
9	Johnny Herbert	GB	Jaguar R1-Cosworth V10		+2 laps
10	Heinz-Harald Frentzen	D	Jordan EJ10-Mugen V10		+8 laps

Retirements		Nat	Car	Laps	Reason
Jos Verstappen		NL	Arrows A21-Supertec V10	60	accident
Michael Schumacher		D	Ferrari F1 2000-Ferrari V10	55	exhaust/rear suspension
Ricardo Zonta		BR	BAR 002-Honda V10	48	accident
Ralf Schumacher		D	Williams FW22-BMW V10	37	accident
Jarno Trulli		I	Jordan EJ10-Mugen V10	36	gearbox
Pedro Diniz		BR	Sauber C19-Petronas V10	30	accident
Jean Alesi		F	Prost AP03-Peugeot V10	29	transmission
Gaston Mazzacane		RA	Minardi M02-Fondmetal V10	22	accident
Marc Gené		E	Minardi M02-Fondmetal V10	21	gearbox
Alexander Wurz		A	Benetton B200-Playlife V10	18	accident
Jenson Button		GB	Williams FW22-BMW V10	16	oil pressure
Pedro de la Rosa		E	Arrows A21-Supertec V10	0	accident at second start

FASTEST LAP M Hakkinen 1m21.571s lap 57 (92.416mph/148.729kmh)

DRIVERS' CHAMPIONSHIP

1	Michael Schumacher	46
2	David Coulthard	34
3	Mika Hakkinen	29
4	Rubens Barrichello	22
5	Giancarlo Fisichella	14
6	Ralf Schumacher	12
7	Heinz-Harald Frentzen	5
	Jacques Villeneuve	5
9	Jarno Trulli	4
10	Jenson Button	3
	Eddie Irvine	3
	Mika Salo	3
12	Pedro de la Rosa	1
	Ricardo Zonta	1

CONSTRUCTORS' CHAMPIONSHIP

1	Ferrari	68
2	McLaren-Mercedes	63
3	Williams-BMW	15
4	Benetton-Playlife	14
5	Jordan-Mugen	9
6	BAR-Honda	6
7	Jaguar	3
	Sauber-Petronas	3
9	Arrows-Supertec	1

GRAND PRIX AIR CANADA

COULTHARD PUTS SCHUEY UNDER THE COSH BY GOING ALMOST AS FAST AS HIM – UNTIL JUST BEFORE THE START OF THE RACE, THAT IS, WHEN THE KIND OF MISTAKE YOU SEE FROM BSM VAUXHALL CORSA DRIVERS ENSURED THE FERRARI STAR HAD NO OPPOSITION. HAKKINEN? HE DIDN'T WANT TO COME OUT AND PLAY THIS WEEKEND

Canada not particularly dry: Herr Spray and part-hidden sidekick Barrichello add a little fizz to the post-race festivities. Inset, improbable third-place finisher Fisichella regales the crowd with a story about a salmon he caught a couple of days previously

MICHAEL SCHUMACHER MUST HAVE THOUGHT CHRISTMAS HAD COME EARLY at the start of the parade lap for the Canadian Grand Prix. He was on pole, he knew it was going to rain [which psychologically gave him a head start of several laps] – and then he saw fellow front-row starter David Coulthard, who is always quick in Montreal – stall and have his car started illegally by the McLaren crew as the field set off for its final formation lap.

Inevitably, the Scot received a yellow card in the form of a 10-second stop-go penalty – and that meant the race was as good as over. The German's nearest challenger at that point was home favourite Jacques Villeneuve, 17 seconds back. It was no surprise that Schumacher went on to win – only that he was the first man to have done so from pole position for 13 grands prix.

But what should have been a romp ended with Schumacher taking the flag only a fraction of a second ahead of team-mate Rubens Barrichello, because a faulty sensor slowed the German in the final 10 laps.

His Brazilian sidekick resisted the temptation to sneak a maiden first F1 win and dutifully obeyed team orders. So many gifts to top up the £100,000 or so that dribbles into his bank account every 24 hours... not a bad return, all in all.

Schumacher said: "I'd like to thank Rubens for protecting me. He is a great team-mate and one day I will repay the favour."

He didn't specify whether that might be before he retires. Was it right to impose team orders at this point in the season [and it was early, because England were still in Euro 2000 at this stage]?

Ferrari thought so – and Barrichello took a charitable view. He said: "Our technical director Ross Brawn asked me to drive slowly, but I have no problem backing off to protect Michael. I trust the team and I am sure if I am in front I will be allowed to win."

Barrichello had an interesting race. He swapped places twice with Mika Hakkinen on the first lap before setting off in pursuit of Villeneuve, who had produced a characteristic lightning start from sixth on the grid. The Canadian's BAR was so fast on the

SCHUMACHER SAID: "I'D LIKE TO THANK RUBENS FOR PROTECTING ME. HE IS A GREAT TEAM-MATE AND ONE DAY I WILL REPAY THE FAVOUR." HE DIDN'T SPECIFY WHETHER THAT MIGHT BE BEFORE HE RETIRES

The waterboys: Coulthard leads Villeneuve shortly before the Canadian went mildly loopy in the closing stages of the race. Above, Schuey and the soon-to-be-penalised DC lead Hakkinen at the start

straights that he was able to hold the second Ferrari at bay until the rain came.

McLaren boss Ron Dennis said: "The die was cast when Villeneuve made the aggressive manoeuvres he did at the start. He was in Canada and had nothing to lose, so he had to go for it. I don't think Mika and Rubens were wimps, but Villeneuve was a total mobile chicane."

That was particularly true after the second round of pit stops, when everyone else had noticed it was raining and opted for wet tyres. But not Jacques, oh no. His duff decision condemned him to a third stop, after which his chances of making any mark on the race were slim – although he made quite a mark on Ralf Schumacher when he punted the Williams-BMW out of the race [see sidebar].

JACQUES AND GILLES

Montreal hasn't exactly been kind to Jacques Villeneuve [above]. The track is named after his late father Gilles, who scored his first grand prix win here for Ferrari in 1978, but his progeny is heading the wrong way if he wants to complete a family double.

Villeneuve Jnr finished second here for Williams in 1996 – but has got nowhere near repeating that since. He has been known to crash into the "Welcome to Quebec" banner at the last chicane, but this year he picked on his rivals instead.

A spirited start put him near the front in the early stages, but a misguided tyre choice later dropped him down the field. When he made a hopelessly ambitious attempt to deprive Ralf Schumacher's Williams of ninth place in the closing stages, he punted the German out of the race – and earned himself a reprimand with a 25-second time penalty by way of a side salad..

Villeneuve said: "I was pushing hard to regain some of the places I had lost. Unfortunately I guess I tried a little bit too hard. I said, 'Sorry'. He said, 'You buy the aspirins'."

Villeneuve had tried a similar move on Coulthard the lap before, only to go flying past and off the track.

Coulthard said: "The funniest bit of the race was Jacques. On the previous lap I could hear him coming – and he went straight through and off. I could see what he was psyching himself up to do and I thought, 'Here we go'. He hit Schumacher at a fair whack. He didn't brake and would have hit the barrier if he hadn't hit Ralf. Ten out of ten for effort, but for common sense..."

Talking of which, DC later took Alexander Wurz's Benetton out of the race – although he had the good grace to stick his hand up and admit culpability. He hadn't seen him, apparently, which was fair enough as little was seen of the Austrian during most of the season.

COULTHARD WAS STEAMED UP ABOUT THE FIA'S DECISION TO PENALISE HIM. "THIS 'LETTER OF THE LAW' ATTITUDE TURNS PEOPLE OFF"

It earned him a ticking-off from the FIA, who also called Pedro Diniz in for a bollocking for squeezing namesake de la Rosa out of the contest. "I admit it didn't look very nice on the TV," Diniz said.

By way of compensation for Arrows, de la Rosa's team-mate Jos Verstappen took fifth – the team's best result for two seasons. The Dutchman's performance at the height of the rainstorm was inspired.

Coulthard was steamed up about the FIA's decision to penalise him. He felt he should have been given the benefit of the doubt. "This 'letter of the law' attitude turns people off," he said.

True, it had been a shame for the race, because there had been so little to choose between Schuey and DC during qualifying. McLaren was gifted a second chance to get the Scot back on the pace, mind, because he came into the pits for a scheduled stop at the perfect time to switch to wets. McLaren being McLaren, however, the team went for the more cautious – and frankly plain wrong – dry-tyre option. He was back in within a couple of laps.

Dennis refused to take the blame, but Coulthard said: "The fact is that the scheduled stop was the perfect moment to change, but I should have overruled. I'd rather these things hadn't happened, but then I shouldn't have stalled, we should have put the right tyres on – and as a team we should have done the job correctly."

To illustrate the point, Fisichella – who pitted at the same time as Coulthard and opted for wets – went on to finish third.

Still – it might have been worse for DC – he could have been Eddie Irvine, who was left behind at the start and then said his car "handled like a skateboard". With his Jaguar roaring like a mouse with a sore throat, the Ulsterman summed up his weekend thus: "It was the worst qualifying session, worst start and worst race of my career."

In Canada, Mika Hakkinen never looked like a man motivated to win a third straight world championship – a feat last achieved by Juan Manuel Fangio in the Fifties.

The Finn had spent the previous three races dogged by rumours that he might quit at the end of the season. Wife Erja was pregnant and Hakkinen, we were told, had promised to give up the sport whenever any Hakklings appeared in their Monaco pad.

The Finn desperately wanted to dispel the notion that he had lost his edge, but wasn't doing a very good job of it. Out of sorts in qualifying, when team-mate Coulthard was scrapping with Schuey for pole, Mika was anonymous in the race and finished a distant fourth.

He said: "I feel less pressure and more relaxed this year than I did last, when I was a bit tense at this stage of the season. But maybe that's not a good thing. Maybe that means I will lose this year.

"That doesn't necessarily mean I am a slower driver. I'm still the same person – still flat out. But to push myself to the maximum level every year after year is extremely difficult."

Nonetheless, Hakkinen remained only two points behind Coulthard – and championship leader Michael Schumacher refused to accept there had been a change in the balance of power at McLaren. "Maybe David has become stronger or equal to Mika," he said, "but I want to see consistent proof. He's already done that in the past only to fall back again."

Eye ludicrous: two questions for Mika Hakkinen (top). One, why have you come over all rubbish? Two, given how much money you earn, why don't you buy some decent shades? Above left, Herbert trudges away from his wounded Jaguar

STARTING GRID

3 M Schumacher
1m18.439s

2 Coulthard
1m18.537s

4 Barrichello
1m18.801s

1 Hakkinen
1m18.985s

5 Frentzen
1m19.483s

22 Villeneuve
1m19.544s

6 Trulli
1m19.581s

23 Zonta
1m19.742s

18 de la Rosa
1m19.912s

11 Fisichella
1m19.932s

8 Herbert
1m19.954s

9 R Schumacher
1m20.073s

19 Verstappen
1m 20.107s

12 Wurz
1m20.113s

17 Salo
1m20.445s

7 Irvine
1m20.500s

14 Alesi
1m20.512s

10 Button
1m20.534s

16 Diniz
1m20.692s

20 Gené
1m21.058s

15 Heidfeld
1m 21.680s

21 Mazzacane
1m22.091s

June 18 2000
CIRCUIT GILLES VILLENEUVE, ILE NOTRE DAME, MONTREAL
CIRCUIT LENGTH: 2.747miles / 4.421km

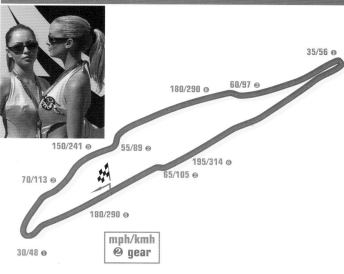

35/56 ❶
180/290 ❻
60/97 ❷
150/241 ❺
55/89 ❷
195/314 ❻
70/113 ❷
65/105 ❷
180/290 ❻
30/48 ❶

mph/kmh
❷ gear

RACE CLASSIFICATION

Pos	Driver	Nat	Car	Laps	Time
1	Michael Schumacher	D	Ferrari F1 2000-Ferrari V10	69	1h41m12.313s
2	Rubens Barrichello	BR	Ferrari F1 2000-Ferrari V10	69	+0.174s
3	Giancarlo Fisichella	I	Benetton B200-Playlife V10	69	+15.365s
4	Mika Hakkinen	FIN	McLaren MP4-15-Mercedes V10	69	+18.561s
5	Jos Verstappen	NL	Arrows A21-Supertec V10	69	+52.208s
6	Jarno Trulli	I	Jordan EJ10-Mugen V10	69	+1m01.687s
7	David Coulthard	GB	McLaren MP4-15-Mercedes V10	69	+1m02.216s
8	Ricardo Zonta	BR	BAR 002-Honda V10	69	+1m10.455s
9	Alexander Wurz	A	Benetton B200-Playlife V10	69	+1m19.899s
10	Pedro Diniz	BR	Sauber C19-Petronas V10	69	+1m29.544s
11	Jenson Button	GB	Williams FW22-BMW V10		+1 lap
12	Gaston Mazzacane	RA	Minardi M02-Fondmetal V10		+1 lap
13	Eddie Irvine	GB	Jaguar R1-Cosworth V10		+3 laps
14	Ralf Schumacher	D	Williams FW22-BMW V10		+5 laps
15	Jacques Villeneuve	CDN	BAR 002-Honda V10		+5 laps
16	Marc Gené	E	Minardi M02-Fondmetal V10		+5 laps

Retirements	Nat	Car	Laps	Reason
Pedro de la Rosa	E	Arrows A21-Supertec V10	48	accident
Mika Salo	FIN	Sauber C19-Petronas V10	42	engine
Jean Alesi	F	Prost AP03-Peugeot V10	38	hydraulics
Nick Heidfeld	D	Prost AP03-Peugeot V10	34	engine
Heinz-Harald Frentzen	D	Jordan EJ10-Mugen V10	32	brakes
Johnny Herbert	GB	Jaguar R1-Cosworth V10	14	gearbox

FASTEST LAP   M Hakkinen 1m19.049s lap 37 (125.106mph/201.338kmh)

DRIVERS' CHAMPIONSHIP

1	Michael Schumacher	56
2	David Coulthard	34
3	Mika Hakkinen	32
4	Rubens Barrichello	28
5	Giancarlo Fisichella	18
6	Ralf Schumacher	12
7	Heinz-Harald Frentzen	5
	Jarno Trulli	5
	Jacques Villeneuve	5
10	Jenson Button	3
	Eddie Irvine	3
	Mika Salo	3
13	Jos Verstappen	2
14	Pedro de la Rosa	1
	Ricardo Zonta	1

CONSTRUCTORS' CHAMPIONSHIP

1	Ferrari	84
2	McLaren-Mercedes	66
3	Benetton-Playlife	18
4	Williams-BMW	15
5	Jordan-Mugen	10
6	BAR-Honda	6
7	Arrows-Supertec	3
	Jaguar	3
	Sauber-Petronas	3

MOBIL 1 GRAND PRIX DE FRANCE

ROLL UP, ROLL UP. GET YOUR NEW COULTHARD HERE. NOW WITH MORE IRON THAN A YEAR'S SUPPLY OF SANATOGEN. FLYING SCOT CUTS A HOLE IN SCHUEY'S LAZIO-TIGHT DEFENCE TO UNDERLINE TITLE CREDENTIALS

Reflected glory: it was a top weekend for DC, all round. Not only did he put one over the obstreperous Captain Scarlet (above), he also had the privilege of spotting a Pin-tailed Sandgrouse – especially rare in eastern central France – on his way to the pits (right). Sadly, points are not awarded for ornithological astuteness

VICTORY NOTWITHSTANDING, DAVID COULTHARD WILL PROBABLY LOOK BACK on France 2000 as a mildly problematic weekend. After overcoming a string of niggles throughout practice and qualifying at Magny-Cours, the Scot came across the biggest obstacle of all in the race. A few clues: he has a red car, a prominent chin and a German passport.

Eventually, however, even Michael Schumacher was swept aside with aplomb as Coulthard took his finest win of the year. And perhaps of his career to that point.

The Scot had been quickest in practice on Friday, but a string of mechanical glitches that were described as "unrelated" [in McLaren jargon, at least] meant he didn't venture out to qualify until more than half of the one-hour session had been run. His own car was still being repaired after a broken fuel pump stopped it in that morning's free practice, so he went out in the spare, which still had team-mate Mika Hakkinen's name plastered all over it.

He aborted one run because Ralf Schumacher inadvertently blocked him, and wasted another because he made a mistake and spun. But finally Coulthard strung together a gung-ho, Hakkinen-style special to qualify three-tenths of a second faster than his team-mate [who, out of sorts, lined up outside the top three for the third race on the trot].

Unfortunately for DC, his best effort still left him slightly slower than Schuey Snr's Ferrari, which zig-zagged unsubtly away from pole position.

As the start lights went out, the German swerved violently in front of Coulthard, who had to back off and thus allowed third-fastest qualifier Rubens Barrichello to nip ahead of him. It was a manoeuvre that set the mood for the race, not to mention the rest of the season.

> **EVEN MICHAEL SCHUMACHER WAS SWEPT ASIDE WITH APLOMB AS COULTHARD TOOK HIS FINEST WIN OF THE YEAR. AND PERHAPS OF HIS CAREER TO THAT POINT**

Chop Schuey: Ferraris to the fore at the start [above], after Schuey swerved across to block Coulthard and paved the way for Barrichello [left] to sweep through and frustrate the McLarens for a bit. Below, Trulli leads the Williams-BMWs of Schuey Jnr and Button in a successful pursuit of the final point

Coulthard said: "Rubens obviously made a good start and was able to go around the outside. But when he did, I didn't try to drive him off the circuit. It wasn't a 'You lift or you're going to crash' scenario."

McLaren boss Ron Dennis added: "I guess if you've got a red car and a certain coloured helmet you expect the sea to open up in front of you."

It took Coulthard 22 laps to get past the Brazilian and set off in search of his main prey. When Hakkinen passed Barrichello courtesy of a scheduled pit stop reshuffle, the leader suddenly had a brace of heated silver arrows pointing directly at his backside – and gaining.

To make things worse for Schuey, his tyres were wearing out far more quickly than those of his key rivals. Coulthard had also set his car up to be especially strong under braking and was preparing to have a pop at Michael at the tight, accident-friendly Adelaide hairpin.

BEAU GESTURE

Many motorists will be familiar with this. You are making serene progress in the third lane of a motorway, passing a line of traffic to your left, when some smug son-of-a-rep in a bright red car [more likely to be a Vauxhall Vectra or BMW 3-series than a Ferrari F1-2000, however] pulls out in front. You brake hard and proffer a selection of hand signals that do not feature in *The Highway Code*.

It is not entirely unusual to see a Formula One driver do this kind of thing mid-race – Pedro Diniz witnesses it almost every other weekend, strangely – but it is rare indeed for David Coulthard to lose his cool. A huge cheer went up in the press gallery when he showed Michael Schumacher exactly what he thought [above] halfway through the French GP.

The Ferrari driver had already pulled one heavy manoeuvre on the Scot at the start, serving across his path in a near-identical move to one he used at Imola. For the next 34 laps Coulthard seethed in his cockpit and set about hunting down the Red Baron. When he finally made an ambitious move round the outside of the hairpin and was repulsed, it all became too much.

Schumacher and Coulthard have something of a history. There was a controversial tangle at Argentina in 1998 and a monstrous accident in Belgium later that year. At Japan in 1999 Schuey was furious because DC, a lap down, held him up for several seconds. Grudges linger.

Coulthard said: "There is a set of rules on the way to drive on the track, and trying to shove people off the circuit is not within them."

After the race Coulthard had to explain his gestures to the FIA. He said: "I apologise if there were children watching, but my emotions were running high..."

HOME DISCOMFORTS

SCHUMACHER DISMISSED COULTHARD'S COMPLAINTS AFTER THE RACE, BUT IT MATTERED LITTLE BECAUSE THERE WAS NOTHING HE COULD DO TO STOP THE McLAREN'S ATTACK

His first attempt was optimistic, to say the least. Schumacher is tough to overtake at the best of times – and the outside line at Adelaide is more easily defendable than most. But given that it's a right-hander, Michael didn't half have to use a lot of left-hand lock to dissuade his pursuer, whose arm came out of the cockpit to signal a gesture of defiance that could clearly be interpreted in the 237 [or however many it is nowadays] countries watching live on TV [see sidebar].

Coulthard said: "It was an exhausting weekend with a lot of problems. That's why I reacted the way I did when Michael tried to drive me off. We all know when we are being sporting and when we are not. You've got to be able to trust people you're racing with because you're risking your life."

Schumacher dismissed Coulthard's complaints after the race, but it mattered little because there was nothing he could do to stop the McLaren's next attack and DC sailed into the distance to claim 10 points.

Hakkinen lined up to challenge Schuey, too, but he simply didn't have Coulthard's angry-young-man-in-a-hurry demeanour and sat behind for 20 laps before finally taking second place. And within a lap of that the German pulled off with a Ferrari engine failure that is almost as rare nowadays as a controversy-free race.

Filling up the points were Jacques Vìlleneuve, who made a characteristically strong start from seventh on the grid, Ralf Schumacher and Jarno Trulli, who incensed Jordan team-mate Heinz-Harald Frentzen by passing him with an uncompromising lunge that led to the two cars touching at the narrow Lycée right-hander.

Wonder where he got that idea?

It is not necessarily an advantage to be racing on home soil. For proof, ask Alain Prost [if you can ever get hold of the beleaguered Frenchman nowadays]. As a driver he won his home grand prix six times in 13 attempts, but as a team manager...

This was never going to be a vintage race for Prost GP, which was in the middle of its worst season since the four-times former champion took the team over in 1997. But things reached new lows at Magny-Cours.

Not known for diplomacy towards engine supplier Peugeot, with whom his deal was about to end, Prost hit out at the company's brand-new EVO4 V10 during qualifying. The result of his gun-pointed-at-own-foot outburst was that Peugeot's engineers went on strike during Sunday's warm-up. The company then went on to withdraw the new engine, which was 10bhp more potent than its forebear.

Driver Jean Alesi sided with Prost during the squabble and went on to have one of those afternoons that only ever seems to happen to him. At the Adelaide hairpin he was hit in two separate incidents – firstly by Marc Gené [and Jean racing against Minardis tells you how bad things were] and later by his Prost team-mate Nick Heidfeld.

He finished 14th, two laps down, but sadly left the track without saying anything, because he's usually quite funny in such circumstances [even if he doesn't mean to be].

Prost-nasal depression: team boss feels the heat [above] after engine supplier Peugeot partook in the French national sport – striking – just because Alain had slagged them off in public. Above left, Schuey Jnr secures a second picture slot in the space of as many pages by doing something photogenic [ie spinning off]

STARTING GRID

3 M Schumacher
1m15.632s

2 Coulthard
1m15.734s

4 Barrichello
1m16.047s

1 Hakkinen
1m16.050s

9 R Schumacher
1m16.291s

7 Irvine
1m16.399s

22 Villeneuve
1m16.653s

5 Frentzen
1m16.658s

6 Trulli
1m16.669s

10 Button
1m16.905s

8 Herbert
1m17.176s

17 Salo
1m17.223s

18 de la Rosa
1m17.279s

11 Fisichella
1m17.317s

16 Diniz
1m17.361s

15 Heidfeld
1m17.374s

12 Wurz
1m17.408s

14 Alesi
1m17.569s

23 Zonta
1m17.668s

19 Verstappen
1m17.933s

20 Gené
1m18.130s

21 Mazzacane
1m18.302s

July 2 2000
CIRCUIT DE NEVERS MAGNY-COURS
CIRCUIT LENGTH: 2.641miles / 4.251km

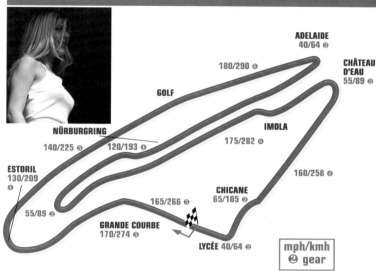

ADELAIDE
40/64 ②

CHÂTEAU
D'EAU
55/89 ④

180/290 ⑥

GOLF

CHÂTEAU

NÜRBURGRING
140/225 ⑤

120/193 ④

IMOLA
175/282 ⑥

ESTORIL
130/209
④

160/258 ④

CHICANE
65/105 ②

165/266 ⑤

55/89 ②

GRANDE COURBE
170/274 ⑤

LYCÉE 40/64 ②

mph/kmh
② gear

RACE CLASSIFICATION

Pos	Driver	Nat	Car	Laps	Time
1	David Coulthard	GB	McLaren MP4-15-Mercedes V10	72	1h38m05.538s
2	Mika Hakkinen	FIN	McLaren MP4-15-Mercedes V10	72	+14.748s
3	Rubens Barrichello	BR	Ferrari F1 2000-Ferrari V10	72	+32.409s
4	Jacques Villeneuve	CDN	BAR 002-Honda V10	72	+1m01.322s
5	Ralf Schumacher	D	Williams FW22-BMW V10	72	+1m03.981s
6	Jarno Trulli	I	Jordan EJ10-Mugen V10	72	+1m15.604s
7	Heinz-Harald Frentzen	D	Jordan EJ10-Mugen V10		+1 lap
8	Jenson Button	GB	Williams FW22-BMW V10		+1 lap
9	Giancarlo Fisichella	I	Benetton B200-Playlife V10		+1 lap
10	Mika Salo	FIN	Sauber C19-Petronas V10		+1 lap
11	Pedro Diniz	BR	Sauber C19-Petronas V10		+1 lap
12	Nick Heidfeld	D	Prost AP03-Peugeot V10		+1 lap
13	Eddie Irvine	GB	Jaguar R1-Cosworth V10		+2 laps
14	Jean Alesi	F	Prost AP03-Peugeot V10		+2 laps
15	Marc Gené	E	Minardi M02-Fondmetal V10		+2 laps

Retirements	Nat	Car	Laps	Reason
Michael Schumacher	D	Ferrari F1 2000-Ferrari V10	58	engine
Pedro de la Rosa	E	Arrows A21-Supertec V10	45	gearbox
Alexander Wurz	A	Benetton B200-Playlife V10	34	spin
Gaston Mazzacane	RA	Minardi M02-Fondmetal V10	31	spin
Jos Verstappen	NL	Arrows A21-Supertec V10	25	gearbox
Johnny Herbert	GB	Jaguar R1-Cosworth V10	20	gearbox
Ricardo Zonta	BR	BAR 002-Honda V10	16	brakes/accident

FASTEST LAP D Coulthard 1m19.479s lap 28 (119.644mph/192.549kmh)

DRIVERS' CHAMPIONSHIP

1	Michael Schumacher	56
2	David Coulthard	44
3	Mika Hakkinen	38
4	Rubens Barrichello	32
5	Giancarlo Fisichella	18
6	Ralf Schumacher	14
7	Jacques Villeneuve	8
8	Jarno Trulli	6
9	Heinz-Harald Frentzen	5
10	Jenson Button	3
	Eddie Irvine	3
	Mika Salo	3
13	Jos Verstappen	2
14	Pedro de la Rosa	1
	Ricardo Zonta	1

CONSTRUCTORS' CHAMPIONSHIP

1	Ferrari	88
2	McLaren-Mercedes	82
3	Benetton-Playlife	18
4	Williams-BMW	17
5	Jordan-Mugen	11
6	BAR-Honda	9
7	Arrows-Supertec	3
	Jaguar	3
	Sauber-Petronas	3

GROSSER A1 PREIS VON ÖSTERREICH

RUMOUR HAD IT THAT MIKA HAKKINEN WAS ALL WASHED UP. HIS RESPONSE? A BLISTERING DRIVE THAT LEFT MOST OF HIS RIVALS FAR IN HIS WAKE. ALL EXCEPT MICHAEL SCHUMACHER, THAT IS. HE WAS IN A GRAVEL TRAP

Massaging a bottle: Barrichello looks on in admiration (above) at McLaren's formation champagne drinking team. Below, Hakkinen and Coulthard sprint away at the first corner as a couple of clumsy pillocks in Ferraris start to lose their bearings

THE FINN WAS SUPPOSED TO BE FINISHED. HE HAD ALLEGEDLY LOST HIS MARBLES.
His motivation, critics whispered, was threadbare. Mika Hakkinen was reportedly preoccupied with the lines on his wife's expanding stomach rather than those on the racetrack. He was even rumoured to be giving up at the end of the season.

Before the start of the Austrian Grand Prix, some bookmakers were offering odds of 8-1 against him winning the world championship.

But it didn't take long for him to prove he had been taking the Mika all along.

After his spell in the doldrums, the McLaren star arrived in Austria refreshed by a week's holiday and produced a performance that outclassed everyone. Most significantly, Hakkinen put one over upstart team-mate David Coulthard. The Scotsman might have left the A1-Ring still two points clear of the Finn, but his sidekick had made it brutally clear that he considered himself to be the main weapon in McLaren's armoury.

The Finn returned to the front of the grid in emphatic fashion. He took pole by four tenths of a second – despite missing much of practice. And it only got better from then on as he crushed the opposition.

"This was a fantastic race for me," he said. "My style of driving didn't suit the set-up we had in Monaco or Canada, so I discussed it very carefully with the engineers and finally we got it sorted. It was a combination of setting up the car, me having some time off, getting my act together and concentrating on the grand prix 100 per cent."

As if he needed anything else, Ferrari also handed him one of the biggest favours he is likely to receive in his career. Michael Schumacher had been below par all weekend and was beaten to third on the grid by team-mate Rubens Barrichello. "They should swap places," Coulthard said, playfully bringing Schuey's zig-zag starts into the mix, "because Michael is bound to end up on that side of the grid anyway."

Perhaps the Brazilian took the comment to heart. Schumacher made a modest start from fourth but, as the Ferrari pair followed the McLarens into the first corner, Barrichello hesitated as if to give way. "We are team-mates working for Ferrari and I didn't want to create any problem for Michael," he said.

It was great planning in every respect, except that both were hit from behind – Barrichello by Jarno Trulli's Jordan, Schumacher by Ricardo Zonta's BAR.

"Michael was on a really tight inside line and almost came to a stop as he was turning," Zonta said. "I braked as hard as I could but touched the back of his car." He also got a stop-go penalty for his troubles.

Trulli added: "I saw Barrichello in front of me braking very early and suddenly everyone seemed to come together."

Sauber's Pedro Diniz added to the general carnage by forgetting that you need to brake for Turn One in Austria. The Brazilian piled into the bewildered Giancarlo Fisichella and shoved the

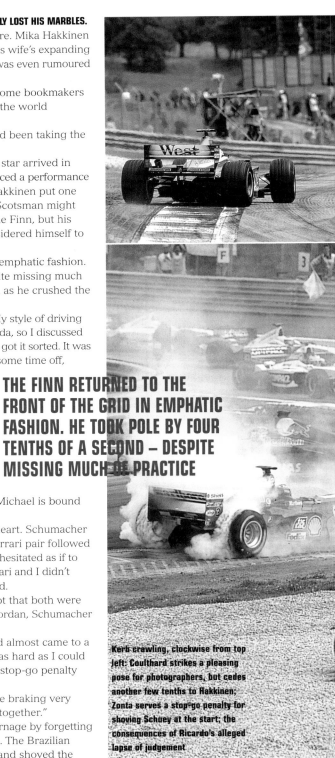

THE FINN RETURNED TO THE FRONT OF THE GRID IN EMPHATIC FASHION. HE TOOK POLE BY FOUR TENTHS OF A SECOND – DESPITE MISSING MUCH OF PRACTICE

Kerb crawling, clockwise from top left: Coulthard strikes a pleasing pose for photographers, but cedes another few tenths to Hakkinen; Zonta serves a stop-go penalty for shoving Schuey at the start; the consequences of Ricardo's alleged lapse of judgement

SEAL BLUBBING

Things are seldom as they seem in Formula One. Hours after Mika Hakkinen [above] scored his most important win of the season, the result was thrown into doubt.

Stewards found that one of the mandatory seals was missing from his car's box of electronics. The result was suspended while the suspect item was taken to the FIA offices to be examined, to make sure there had been no tampering and that the software matched the original blueprint. It did, so Hakkinen was allowed to keep his 10 points for victory. By way of punishment, however, McLaren was stripped of its points in the championship for constructors. It alleged the seal had fallen off simply because of excessive vibration.

Team boss Ron Dennis was later incensed to hear that Ferrari had sent a letter to the stewards, to outline all the technical trickery that could have taken place with the seal missing. Other teams are traditionally not allowed to play a part in investigations of this sort until it goes to appeal.

Ferrari technical director Ross Brawn pointed out that his team sent the letter in order to speed up the investigative process. He said: "Theoretically if the seal is broken you can access software the FIA has installed to prevent cheating. Last year, it was Ron who said teams could write self-modifying codes that could disappear and never be traced.

"Our move wasn't Machiavellian, or anything dodgy, but I guess one or two people are getting a bit emotional about it."

He didn't quite get the words "emotion" and "McLaren into the same sentence – that really would have been a first.

BAPTISM OF MIRE

No Formula One debut is ever easy, but Luciano Burti's first grand prix was tougher than most.

The Brazilian learned he would be driving for Jaguar less than 48 hours before the start of the Austrian GP, because Eddie Irvine withdrew on Friday afternoon after complaining of severe abdominal pains.

Burti assumed it was all a big wind-up... until he found himself staying at the circuit until midnight to pass all the FIA safety tests.

He should have had two sessions on Saturday to learn the circuit and get ready for qualifying, but there are occasional drawbacks to driving for Jaguar. A blown clutch early on Saturday morning left him with precious little chance to acclimatise.

Burti said: "The problems didn't matter too much – I knew it would be hard learning the track in an hour and a half on Saturday morning, so the fact I only got 45 minutes only made it a bit more difficult."

He later followed countryman Rubens Barrichello round to learn the line and went on to qualify 21st, ahead of Gaston Mazzacane. He made his first practice pit stop on Sunday morning – and things were starting to look a little more organised until a couple of minutes before the start, when his car broke. And the spare was set up for imp-sized team-mate Johnny Herbert.

"Johnny is shorter than me and the pedals were too close, which was painful," Burti said. "I knew I wouldn't get a great result starting from the back, so I just tried to finish."

Which, somehow, he did. Seldom has a 12th place been so hard earned.

Sharp Arrows: de la Rosa [top left] held a solid third initially. Above, Burti was a last-minute substitute for Jaguar

DE LA ROSA KEPT PACE WITH COULTHARD FOR THE FIRST HALF OF THE RACE, UNTIL A "50p PIPE" IN HIS ARROWS' OIL COOLER FORCED HIM OUT

Italian out of the contest. Benetton boss Flavio Briatore said: "It was an incredible manoeuvre – not at all professional for someone in F1."

It certainly wasn't as slick as Schuey's thinking. The German's car came to a halt minus its front wing but, ever the opportunist, he restarted before stopping almost as soon as he regained the circuit, with his car parked sideways across the track. He got out, no doubt thinking he had done enough to get the race stopped, but the authorities kept their red flags firmly under wraps and sent out the Safety Car.

With Schuey sidelined and Barrichello delayed, the race promised a glimpse of potential glory for some of those who traditionally play only supporting roles. Mika Salo picked his way through the first-corner mess to grab third on the opening lap, but he soon lost out to Pedro de la Rosa. The Spaniard kept pace with Coulthard for the first half of the race, until a "50p pipe" in his Arrows' oil cooler broke and forced him out.

In the end, Barrichello recovered to make the podium – despite having sustained a broken floor at the start. Jacques Villeneuve stormed back from an early 15th place, when he was bottled up behind Nick Heidfeld's Prost, to take his second consecutive fourth place. He was actually delayed by Heidfeld for 40 laps, during which he grew predictably more irate. "He was driving as though he was in Formula 3000, just putting everyone on the grass," Villeneuve said.

In the end, Heidfeld finished up on the grass after tangling with team-mate Jean Alesi – the second consecutive race in which they had collided. This time, they both retired. Small wonder that Alain Prost was rumoured to be selling up.

STARTING GRID

1 Hakkinen 1m10.410s
2 Coulthard 1m10.795s
4 Barrichello 1m10.844s
3 M Schumacher 1m11.046s
6 Trulli 1m11.640s
23 Zonta 1m11.647s
22 Villeneuve 1m11.649s
11 Fisichella 1m11.658s
17 Salo 1m11.761s
19 Verstappen 1m11.905s
16 Diniz 1m11.931s
18 de la Rosa 1m11.978s
15 Heidfeld 1m12.037s
12 Wurz 1m12.038s
5 Frentzen 1m12.043s
8 Herbert 1m12.238s
14 Alesi 1m12.304s
10 Button 1m12.337s
9 R Schumacher 1m12.347s
20 Gené 1m12.722s
7 Burti 1m12.822s
21 Mazzacane 1m13.419s

July 16 2000
A1-RING, SPIELBERG
CIRCUIT LENGTH: 2.688miles / 4.326km

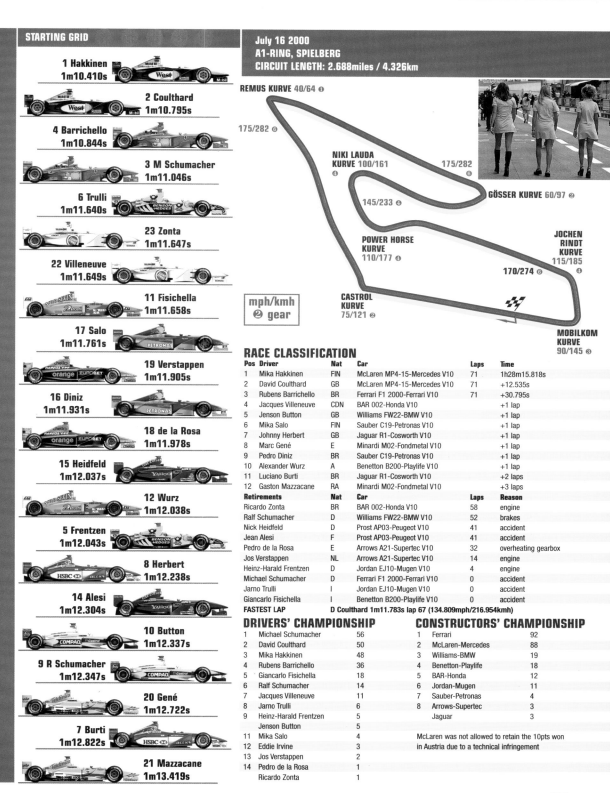

REMUS KURVE 40/64 ❶
175/282 ❻
NIKI LAUDA KURVE 100/161 ❹
175/282 ❻
145/233 ❹
GÖSSER KURVE 60/97 ❷
POWER HORSE KURVE 110/177 ❹
JOCHEN RINDT KURVE 115/185 ❶
170/274 ❻
CASTROL KURVE 75/121 ❷
MOBILKOM KURVE 90/145 ❸

mph/kmh
❷ gear

RACE CLASSIFICATION

Pos	Driver	Nat	Car	Laps	Time
1	Mika Hakkinen	FIN	McLaren MP4-15-Mercedes V10	71	1h28m15.818s
2	David Coulthard	GB	McLaren MP4-15-Mercedes V10	71	+12.535s
3	Rubens Barrichello	BR	Ferrari F1 2000-Ferrari V10	71	+30.795s
4	Jacques Villeneuve	CDN	BAR 002-Honda V10		+1 lap
5	Jenson Button	GB	Williams FW22-BMW V10		+1 lap
6	Mika Salo	FIN	Sauber C19-Petronas V10		+1 lap
7	Johnny Herbert	GB	Jaguar R1-Cosworth V10		+1 lap
8	Marc Gené	E	Minardi M02-Fondmetal V10		+1 lap
9	Pedro Diniz	BR	Sauber C19-Petronas V10		+1 lap
10	Alexander Wurz	A	Benetton B200-Playlife V10		+1 lap
11	Luciano Burti	BR	Jaguar R1-Cosworth V10		+2 laps
12	Gaston Mazzacane	RA	Minardi M02-Fondmetal V10		+3 laps

Retirements	Nat	Car	Laps	Reason
Ricardo Zonta	BR	BAR 002-Honda V10	58	engine
Ralf Schumacher	D	Williams FW22-BMW V10	52	brakes
Nick Heidfeld	D	Prost AP03-Peugeot V10	41	accident
Jean Alesi	F	Prost AP03-Peugeot V10	41	accident
Pedro de la Rosa	E	Arrows A21-Supertec V10	32	overheating gearbox
Jos Verstappen	NL	Arrows A21-Supertec V10	14	engine
Heinz-Harald Frentzen	D	Jordan EJ10-Mugen V10	4	engine
Michael Schumacher	D	Ferrari F1 2000-Ferrari V10	0	accident
Jarno Trulli	I	Jordan EJ10-Mugen V10	0	accident
Giancarlo Fisichella	I	Benetton B200-Playlife V10	0	accident

FASTEST LAP D Coulthard 1m11.783s lap 67 (134.809mph/216.954kmh)

DRIVERS' CHAMPIONSHIP

1	Michael Schumacher	56
2	David Coulthard	50
3	Mika Hakkinen	48
4	Rubens Barrichello	36
5	Giancarlo Fisichella	18
6	Ralf Schumacher	14
7	Jacques Villeneuve	11
8	Jarno Trulli	6
9	Heinz-Harald Frentzen	5
	Jenson Button	5
11	Mika Salo	4
12	Eddie Irvine	3
13	Jos Verstappen	2
14	Pedro de la Rosa	1
	Ricardo Zonta	1

CONSTRUCTORS' CHAMPIONSHIP

1	Ferrari	92
2	McLaren-Mercedes	88
3	Williams-BMW	19
4	Benetton-Playlife	18
5	BAR-Honda	12
6	Jordan-Mugen	11
7	Sauber-Petronas	4
8	Arrows-Supertec	3
	Jaguar	3

McLaren was not allowed to retain the 10pts won
in Austria due to a technical infringement

TIME IS WEIRD. AS A YOUNGSTER, THE HOUR AND A BIT YOU had to wait after tea on a Sunday evening to watch the edited Formula One highlights seemed to drag on forever. To an adult, that same hour and a bit appears to come and go faster than you can say, "What the hell is a Gaston Mazzacane?"

To musicians, time is a multi-faceted concept that has served up a million and one song titles, from Time Boom X De Devil Dead, by the not-at-all-barking Lee 'Scratch' Perry, to Time is Tight [Booker T & the MGs] via Time and a Word [splendid warbling nonsense by Yes, a popular staple in sixth-form common rooms up and down the country in the early Seventies].

To us, it is merely something that passes too bloody quickly. It barely seems yesterday that centre throttle pedals were all the rage, Jackie Stewart wore corduroy caps, Formula One cars had suspension that moved and Jacques Villeneuve had hair.

Please join us on a trip back through the years as we celebrate some of the [mostly] motor sporting landmarks – some happy, some sad – that made us feel old during the past season.

70 YEARS AGO/1930

OCT 28: Bernie Ecclestone [1] emerges on Planet Earth, in St Peters, Suffolk. He subsequently fails to qualify for either of the two grands prix he enters, although he fares respectably in other business ventures.

60 YEARS AGO/1940

JAN 18: Pedro Rodriguez [2] born. A great natural talent, the Mexican's CV does not fully reflect his ability. At home in any kind of car and a master of the fearsome Porsche 917 [3], he perished while racing a Ferrari for the fun of it in a meaningless sports car race in 1971.

FEB 21: Peter Gethin [5] born... probably at a slower speed than the 150.755mph average at which he won the 1971 Italian GP [main photo]. His only world championship race success wasn't just the fastest in history – it was also the closest. He beat Ronnie Peterson by 0.01 seconds.

FEB 28: Mario Andretti [4] born. Four times a winner of America's premier Champ Car series, he took the F1 title with Lotus in 1978 and is still trying to win Le Mans, even though the fastest most people of his age usually travel is when they use their free bus pass.

YESTERDAY

ONCE MORE

50 YEARS AGO/1950

JAN 18: Gilles Villeneuve [1] born. A deity on four wheels and father of 1997 world champion Jacques, he used to drive crap cars faster than they were designed to go. He only won six grands prix before his death at Zolder in 1982. That was the last time the editor of this book can remember having cried.

JAN 29: Jody Scheckter born. The South African turned from serial crasher into consummate race finisher and became world champion for Ferrari in 1979. Still hanging around the tracks with sons Toby and Tomas. Good news, Jody: you don't actually look 50...

MAY 13: World championship motor racing began on an airfield not far from what we nowadays know as the A43. Silverstone thinks its facilities have improved since; some might beg to differ. Giuseppe Farina won for Alfa Romeo [7]; team-mate Juan Manuel Fangio retired with a broken con-rod.

MAY 21: Fangio scores his first world championship win in Monaco. Alberto Ascari is second, a lap in arrears, on the occasion of Ferrari's first GP start.

SEP 3: Giuseppe Farina clinches the first-ever world title by winning the Italian GP at Monza.

45 YEARS AGO/1955

JUL 16: Stirling Moss heads team-mate Juan Manuel Fangio in a Mercedes 1-2 at Aintree [4] to win the British GP and score his first F1 championship success.

40 YEARS AGO/1960

MAR 21: Ayrton Senna born. Went on to be quite good.

APR 1: Loris Kessel born. Went on to be hopeless, but did try to enter a knackered old Williams for a couple of races in 1977, which was quite funny. He called it an Apollon. It was rubbish.

MAY 29: Privateer Stirling Moss gives Lotus its first GP win in Monaco. Former motorcycle world champion John Surtees makes his championship debut with the works team, but retires with transmission trouble.

JUN 2: Marque founder Bruce McLaren perishes in a testing accident at Goodwood.

JUN 6: Jim Clark starts his first GP for Team Lotus [trailing Graham Hill's BRM, **8**]. He lines up 11th of 21, but transmission troubles put him out – as was fashionable for Lotus rookies at the time.

JUL 3: The Vanwall marque starts its final grand prix in France [**2**]. Less than two years earlier it had collected the inaugural world championship for constructors.

SEP 17: Future motorcycle courier and punk guitarist Damon [**3**] becomes the second child of F1 driver Graham Hill and his wife Bette.

NOV 20: Privateer Bob Drake finishes 13th in the American GP at Riverside – it's his only GP start, but it marks Maserati's 69th and last as a chassis builder.

35 YEARS AGO/1965

JAN 1: Jackie Stewart starts his first grand prix in South Africa and takes his BRM to sixth place. It was the last F1 championship race to take place at East London [which, for those who thought this meant Chingford, is actually in Cape Province].

30 YEARS AGO/1970

MAR 7: Triple world champion Jack [now Sir Jack] Brabham scores his final GP win in South Africa at the start of his final season. Jackie Stewart gives ambitious new company March [**5**] a promising third place in its first world championship start.

MAY 10: Spectacular Swede Ronnie Peterson starts his first world championship race at Monaco in a March 701 [**6**] entered by the snappily named Antique Automobiles

Racing Team. Despite the weight handicap imposed by having to carry such big stickers, he finishes seventh.

MAY 22: Pedro Diniz chugs into the world.

MAY 22 AND 5 MINUTES: Pedro Diniz causes first accident [shot in the dark, this one – might not be quite right, but we strongly suspect he probably nutted the midwife].

JUNE: Yes release Time and a Word, their second LP. So many afghan-wearing students and self-labelled musical experts in form 3B rush out to buy it that it sprints [sort of] to number 45 in the UK album charts.

AUG 2: Hockenheim stages its first F1 GP. Unfortunately, it wasn't the last.

SEP 5: Jochen Rindt [**4**] dies from injuries sustained in a practice crash at Monza. He goes on to be the sport's first posthumous world champion.

SEP 20: A Tyrrell car makes its first GP start in Canada. Jackie Stewart qualifies it on pole, but a broken stub axle forces him out.

25 YEARS AGO/1975

JAN 26: Graham Hill starts his 176th and last world championship GP in Brazil. He finished 12th in his self-entered Lola T370.

JUN 22: James Hunt wins his first – and Hesketh's only – grand prix at Zandvoort, Holland [**8**]. The event clashed with a fantastically exciting autocross meeting in Middlewich, Cheshire. Not many people know this.

NOV 29: Little more than four months after announcing his definitive retirement from the sport, Graham Hill dies when his light plane crashes on Elstree golf course. His passengers also perish. One of them is Tony Brise [**6**], a rising star in the racing firmament.

20 YEARS AGO/1980

JAN 13: Alain Prost starts his first grand prix in Argentina and takes his McLaren M29 to sixth place [**1**]. He goes on to

be rather better at this side of the business than he would prove to be at team management.

AUG 17: Nigel Mansell starts his first F1 race for Team Lotus in Austria [**2**]. He gets soaked in petrol, but comes back for more nonetheless.

15 YEARS AGO/1985

APR 7: In Brazil, Minardi arrives in F1 [**3**] with a car that weighs almost as much as the other 24 on the grid put together. The Italian team has since started more than 250 races... but scored rather fewer points.

APR 21: Ayrton Senna scores his first GP win for Lotus in teeming rain at Estoril [greeted by team director Peter Warr, **9**].

JUL 7: Nelson Piquet gives Brabham its 35th – and last – F1 success at Paul Ricard, France [**5**].

NOV 3: Triple champion Niki Lauda takes part in his 171st and final GP in Adelaide, Australia.

10 YEARS AGO/1990

OCT 21: Ayrton Senna misses out on a possible seventh win of the season when he tangles with arch-rival Alain Prost at the start of the Japanese GP. The shunt, which the Brazilian eventually admits was deliberate, clinches the McLaren star's second world title.

5 YEARS AGO/1995

OCT 22: Michael Schumacher [**7**] clinches his second world title in Japan. At 26, he becomes F1's youngest double champion.

GROSSER MOBIL 1 PREIS VON DEUTSCHLAND

RUBENS BARRICHELLO SCORES HIS
MAIDEN GP SUCCESS IN A RACE WITH
MORE INCIDENT THAN A DECADE OF ENGLAND
SOCCER INTERNATIONALS. AND HIS BRIO
PRESERVED TEAM-MATE SCHUEY'S POINTS LEAD
JUST AS THE GERMAN WAS DEVELOPING A
REAL TASTE FOR FIRST-CORNER PILE-UPS

Brazilian goes nuts: have you ever seen Häkkinen
and Coulthard celebrate like this with Schuey after a
GP (above). No, we haven't either. Below, Zonta leads
Ralf Schumacher, Wurz, Heidfeld and Barrichello into
the first chicane on lap one. By this stage the Brazilian
had gained five places, so only another 12 to go...

GO ON, ADMIT IT. YOU HAD A TEAR IN YOUR EYE, TOO. THE SIGHT OF RUBENS Barrichello grizzling on the podium after winning his first grand prix [at the 123rd attempt] will live long in racing fans' memories. And the circumstances surrounding his success might endure even longer.

Ferrari's "sacrificial lamb" [© a managerial type at McLaren who looks not dissimilar to former Chelsea, Man Utd and England midfielder Butch Wilkins] stormed through from 18th on the grid, thanks to a blend of his own brio and the odd lucky break along the way. Not even the most optimistic race strategist could have accounted for this weekend's Formula One innovation, the stray nutter [see sidebar].

Barrichello has always shone in mixed wet/dry conditions of the kind that prevailed at Hockenheim. And a stint on dry tyres in the rain at the end of the race ultimately won him the chance to stand on the top step, dedicate his victory to late mentor Ayrton Senna and blub uncontrollably. These were tears of real joy.

The Brazilian had rather different reasons for weeping after the rain-hit qualifying session, because his Ferrari broke and forced him to set his best [relatively speaking] time when conditions were far from ideal. It left him only four places from the back. But race day was different – and the very first lap told you Barrichello was in no mood to hang around, because he was

FERRARI'S "SACRIFICIAL LAMB" STORMED THROUGH FROM 18TH ON THE GRID, THANKS TO A BLEND OF HIS OWN BRIO AND THE ODD LUCKY BREAK

Schuey stopper, from top left: thousands of aled-up fans are pitched into despair as their hero comes to grief at the start; Hakkinen and Coulthard running first and second; Mika comes in for wets – which was very wrong. Germany [above]: a great place for a summer holiday. Main shot: Barrichello in the solitude of the forest

up to 10th by the end of it. Six laps later he had sliced his way through to fifth and 16th time around he was up to third.

Still, there was a price to pay for spending so much time passing 15 cars: the Brazilian was 14 seconds adrift of race leader Mika Hakkinen by the time he breached the top three. Besides, Rubens – who had started on a relatively light fuel load, to facilitate passing manoeuvres – faced two scheduled pit stops, while the pace-setting Finn had but one to make. When Barrichello came in for the first time, he dropped to sixth.

But it wasn't long before some nutcase breached circuit security and started ambling along by the trackside. Cue the Safety Car. It was only eight laps since Barrichello's first stop, but he promptly came in again and took on enough fuel to make it to the finish. This unexpected turn of events put Barrichello third, now on the same strategy as everyone else, with half the race to go.

Third soon became second when Jordan's Jarno Trulli was called in for a stop-go penalty for allegedly having overtaken the Ferrari while the Safety Car was still operational. [Ferrari team boss Jean Todt alleged as much, anyway, and someone believed him, although Trulli was flummoxed.]

When rain started falling heavily late in the race, Hakkinen was among those who opted to come in for wets. Barrichello, however, insisted on staying out on a track that was sodden in some parts – but almost bone dry in others. His gamble paid off handsomely.

Barrichello said: "Our technical director Ross Brawn told

A WALK ON THE WILD SIDE

Even after queuing for several hours to escape a Silverstone car park, F1 fans are usually happy at the end of their big sporting day out. Come rain or shine, they'll have something to tell the grandchildren one day, even if only that they had been there. But simply "being there" wasn't enough for one fan in Germany.

Halfway through the race a bloke in a white raincoat was seen wandering beside the track. As cars were doing about 200mph at that point, the Safety Car [above] was promptly put out so that better adjusted men in white coats could capture and remove the intruder.

Frenchman Robert Selhi, 47, was later identified as the man who changed the face of the 2000 German GP. Covered in slogans that weren't readily identifiable via the TV screen, he was protesting about what he considered to be his unfair dismissal by Mercedes France. But while Selhi's message might not have got across, he certainly succeeded in screwing up Merc's race.

McLaren has never been the sharpest team when it comes to strategy. When Selhi's idiocy sent the Safety Car out it was the ideal time to make a scheduled stop for those originally planning to come in just the once. Hakkinen dived in but Coulthard – who would have lost only several seconds had he queued behind his team-mate to wait for a service – stayed out for another full lap at Safety Car speed, which dropped him almost to the tail of the pack.

Team boss Ron Dennis said: "We led by 20 seconds and there was no scenario that was going to cost us the race. Then this lunatic walks onto the circuit. I don't think any team can predict that. After that we had to be cautious while Barrichello had nothing to lose."

Selhi later apologised. One day, perhaps, his grandchildren will find out that he was there, but not exactly all there.

COULTHARD SWERVED ACROSS SHARPLY TO BLOCK NEIGHBOUR SCHUEY – A CARBON COPY OF THE GERMAN'S TACTICS

me on the radio that I'd win if I could keep up the pace I was running at, and I did. It's been such a long time since I won a race, I'd lost the taste."

For the second time in as many races, Barrichello had received the undying attention of the Ferrari pit, because Michael Schumacher crashed out at the first corner – again – this time after a collision with Benetton's Giancarlo Fisichella. Thanks to Barrichello, however, the German still led the title chase.

Hakkinen was a philosophical second. He had made a dynamite start from fourth on the grid, aided slightly by pole-winning team-mate David Coulthard. The Scot moved sluggishly off the line and swerved across sharply to block neighbour Schuey – a carbon copy of tactics the German had employed earlier in the year. That left a gap, and Hakkinen didn't need asking twice to use it and plunder the lead as they swept into the first turn.

The Finn said: "For the first 10 laps I was in heaven. I was thinking, 'Wow, what a start'. But really I should have been concentrating on my braking points."

Hakkinen thanked the team for "creating a tactic" at the start, but McLaren boss Ron Dennis hastily denied any choreography: "I'm unaware of any deliberate strategy," he said. "How could you predict Michael making a bad start?"

While Schuey joined the post-race celebrations and lauded Barrichello, one driver was notably less enthusiastic about his team-mate. BAR's Jacques Villeneuve was not amused that Ricardo Zonta had clipped him into a spin when both were challenging for points. "His mistake cost us fifth and sixth positions," the Canadian fumed. "I don't have much respect for him as a result."

A THUMPING GOOD IDEA

As the arguments over starting etiquette raged on in Germany, with Michael Schumacher and Giancarlo Fisichella piling into each other at the first corner, a lone voice of sanity stood out. Jean Alesi thought everyone should stop whingeing and have a good, old-fashioned scrap.

Tired of the constant sniping about what is and isn't acceptable in the first 200 metres of a race, Alesi said: "After the drivers' briefing in Austria, we all stayed on for 20 minutes while three drivers fought it out in front of us like kids in a kindergarten, and nothing happened.

"In the days of Ayrton Senna, I remember him going to see Eddie Irvine, who had upset him during the Japanese GP, which was Eddie's first race. They argued and then, at the end, Ayrton punched his nose. For me that was more motor racing. When you have a problem with somebody you need to go to argue with them – not waste time by squabbling at the briefing and obtaining no result."

Alesi's race later ended in "the worst accident of his life". Pedro Diniz failed to spot the Frenchman's Prost alongside him [as you do at 200mph] and moved across. The collision pitched Jean into a violent spin and, subsequently, a massive impact with the barriers. The Frenchman threw down his helmet in anger, but before he could practise what he preached on his former Sauber team-mate, he was overcome by a more pressing need to vomit and so set off into the trees.

He wasn't the only madman in the woods that day, as it happened.

Cage bored: Alesi smoulders behind the fence [above] after being victim of some Diniz GBH. Button, who stalled at the start and was last away, slices inside Villeneuve [top left] en route to fourth

STARTING GRID

2 Coulthard
1m45.697s

3 M Schumacher
1m47.063s

11 Fisichella
1m47.130s

1 Hakkinen
1m47.162s

18 de la Rosa
1m47.786s

6 Trulli
1m47.833s

12 Wurz
1m48.037s

8 Herbert
1m48.078s

22 Villeneuve
1m48.121s

7 Irvine
1m48.305s

19 Verstappen
1m48.321s

23 Zonta
1m48.665s

15 Heidfeld
1m48.690s

9 R Schumacher
1m48.841s

17 Salo
1m49.204s

10 Button
1m49.215s

5 Frentzen
1m49.280s

4 Barrichello
1m49.544s

16 Diniz
1m49.936s

14 Alesi
1m50.289s

21 Mazzacane
1m51.611s

20 Gené
1m53.094s

July 30 2000
HOCKENHEIM-RING, NEAR HEIDELBERG
CIRCUIT LENGTH: 4.241miles / 6.825km

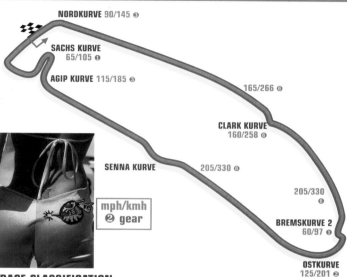

NORDKURVE 90/145 ③

SACHS KURVE 65/105 ①

AGIP KURVE 115/185 ③

165/266 ⑥

CLARK KURVE 160/258 ⑥

SENNA KURVE 205/330 ⑥

205/330 ⑥

BREMSKURVE 2 60/97 ①

OSTKURVE 125/201 ②

mph/kmh
❷ gear

RACE CLASSIFICATION

Pos	Driver	Nat	Car	Laps	Time
1	Rubens Barrichello	BR	Ferrari F1 2000-Ferrari V10	45	1h25m34.418s
2	Mika Hakkinen	FIN	McLaren MP4-15-Mercedes V10	45	+7.452s
3	David Coulthard	GB	McLaren MP4-15-Mercedes V10	45	+21.168s
4	Jenson Button	GB	Williams FW22-BMW V10	45	+22.685s
5	Mika Salo	FIN	Sauber C19-Petronas V10	45	+27.112s
6	Pedro de la Rosa	E	Arrows A21-Supertec V10	45	+29.079s
7	Ralf Schumacher	D	Williams FW22-BMW V10	45	+30.897s
8	Jacques Villeneuve	CDN	BAR 002-Honda V10	45	+47.537s
9	Jarno Trulli	I	Jordan EJ10-Mugen V10	45	+50.901s
10	Eddie Irvine	GB	Jaguar R1-Cosworth V10	45	+1h19.664s
11	Gaston Mazzacane	RA	Minardi M02-Fondmetal V10	45	+1h29.504s
12	Nick Heidfeld	D	Prost AP03-Peugeot V10		+5 laps

Retirements	Nat	Car	Laps	Reason
Heinz-Harald Frentzen	D	Jordan EJ10-Mugen V10	39	electronics
Jos Verstappen	NL	Arrows A21-Supertec V10	39	spin
Ricardo Zonta	BR	BAR 002-Honda V10	37	spin
Marc Gené	E	Minardi M02-Fondmetal V10	33	engine
Alexander Wurz	A	Benetton B200-Playlife V10	31	gearbox/spin
Pedro Diniz	BR	Sauber C19-Petronas V10	29	accident
Jean Alesi	F	Prost AP03-Peugeot V10	29	accident
Johnny Herbert	GB	Jaguar R1-Cosworth V10	12	gearbox
Michael Schumacher	D	Ferrari F1 2000-Ferrari V10	0	accident
Giancarlo Fisichella	I	Benetton B200-Playlife V10	0	accident

FASTEST LAP R Barrichello 1m44.300s lap 20 (146.377mph/235.570kmh)

DRIVERS' CHAMPIONSHIP

1	Michael Schumacher	56
2	David Coulthard	54
	Mika Hakkinen	54
4	Rubens Barrichello	46
5	Giancarlo Fisichella	18
6	Ralf Schumacher	14
7	Jacques Villeneuve	11
8	Jenson Button	8
9	Mika Salo	6
	Jarno Trulli	6
11	Heinz-Harald Frentzen	5
12	Eddie Irvine	3
13	Jos Verstappen	2
	Pedro de la Rosa	2
15	Ricardo Zonta	1

CONSTRUCTORS' CHAMPIONSHIP

1	Ferrari	102
2	McLaren-Mercedes	98
3	Williams-BMW	22
4	Benetton-Playlife	18
5	BAR-Honda	12
6	Jordan-Mugen	11
7	Sauber-Petronas	6
8	Arrows-Supertec	4
9	Jaguar	3

MARLBORO MAGYAR NAGYDIJ

THE 2000 HUNGARIAN GP
LACKED THE CUT-THROAT
DRAMA OF THE AVERAGE
SHEEPDOG TRIAL, BUT YOU
CAN BLAME THE PURITY OF
MIKA HAKKINEN'S RACING
INSTINCTS FOR THAT

Fastest Lapp (sort of): Hakkinen speeds past
Herbert's lumbering XJ6 on his way to giving Schuey
a thorough pasting (main shot). He later gave his
third-placed team-mate a lesson in how to make
rivals' eyes sting with a superior quality of
champagne aim

THE GENERAL CONSENSUS WAS THAT HUNGARY 2000 PROVIDED A DULL RACE of outstanding greyness, but that's to overlook the spark of genius that rendered it so.

True, this was no edge-of-your-seat heart-stopper – although there was always more likelihood of Gaston Mazzacane winning than there was of Budapest matching the previous race in Hockenheim for incident. Even when completely half-cut, as the tens of thousands of Finns and Germans who invade the place tend to be from nine on Thursday morning onwards, they stop short of invading the track while there are cars going round.

This was a dour spectacle because of a five-second burst of inspiration from Mika Hakkinen at the start. The Finn had described his dynamite getaway in Germany as a "once-in-a-season" occurrence – a notion he disproved pretty sharpish.

"Yeah, I lied,"he said later, with a broad grin. "That was two in a row."

Throughout qualifying, the McLarens had looked a strong bet for the race – if only they could get ahead of one pesky Ferrari.

THIS WAS A DOUR SPECTACLE BECAUSE OF A FIVE-SECOND BURST OF INSPIRATION FROM MIKA HAKKINEN AT THE START

McLaren drive-thru: any thoughts Schuey might have had about making his customary first-corner chop were nixed by the flying Hakkinen, who made full use of the afternoon's only viable passing opportunity [aka the start]

DAY TRIP TO BLOCKPOOL

Michael Schumacher's deft touch has counted for a lot in Hungary in the past – remember 1998, when he had to string together about 20 qualifying-style laps on the trot to mince the McLarens?

He missed the race in 1999, of course, while recovering from a broken leg – but memories of his epic win two years previously were still strong and the Ferrari star was expected to shore up his increasingly fragile points lead.

Sure enough, he took pole – but while the Ferrari looked good over a single lap, there were doubts it could preserve its tyres as well as the McLarens in the typically searing mid-summer heat of eastern Europe.

First, however, the silver cars had to get past – which has never been the work of a moment in Hungary.

David Coulthard appeared to have the measure of team-mate Hakkinen in qualifying, but starting on the outside of the front row, the dirtier side of the track, was always going to minimise his chances of outsprinting Schuey to the first turn.

The German made a clean start and duly left Coulthard in his wake – but when he went to claim the inside line for the attractively named Turn One he was startled by a flash of silver as Hakkinen profited from the momentum of his fantastic start from third on the grid and catapulted up the inside. "I tried to make it hard for him," Michael said, "but once I realised where he was I gave him room."

Not that he had much choice in the matter.

Hakkinen began the race on fresh Bridgestones, which took a couple of laps to reach their peak – but once they did, he was gone.

Formula One boss Bernie Ecclestone is adamant. He doesn't want grand prix racing to return to the way it was in the late Eighties, when about 40 cars – many the product of pure reverie rather than anything like a business plan – littered the paddock.

The limit nowadays is 24 – a target that will be reached when Toyota takes up the final two entries in 2002.

To David Coulthard, however, it felt as though there were already at least that many cars on the track in Budapest. "Were there four Minardis out there?" the Scot asked, only half joking, after his pursuit of second place was hindered on a handful of occasions by the perennial tail-enders.

After the final round of pit stops, Coulthard fancied his chances of depriving Michael Schumacher of second place – but wayward lumps of lime-green carbonfibre helped put that slim hope beyond reach.

Minardi, of course, is Italian – and often makes use of Ferrari's private test track at Fiorano. It was perfect fodder for F1's armada of conspiracy theorists – but McLaren boss Ron Dennis stopped short of suggesting anything untoward. "I don't think it was sinister," he said. "Their drivers just need use their mirrors more."

One of the accused, Marc Gené [above], a genuinely decent bloke, said: "It didn't take Coulthard longer to pass me than it did anyone else. You can't just get out of the way within the first couple of seconds. I always try to move over within a lap – and I think that's good enough."

Ironically, the Spaniard was later given a 10-second stop-go penalty for blocking Eddie Irvine. Not unreasonably, given Jaguar's early-season form and a lack of information from his own pit, Marc thought he had been racing him for position.

SOCCER PUNCH

Formula One is enormously popular the globe over, but soccer is even more so – and you don't need expensive gadgets to take part. A ball, a park, a couple of jumpers for goalposts, a couple of like-minded mates and you're away. Costs a bit less than building a McLaren MP4-15.

Until the summer of 2000, however, nobody had discussed cross-breeding the two.

During the recess between Hockenheim and Hungary, Premier 1 Grand Prix was announced. Scheduled for launch in 2002, it is pitched as a rival to F1 in terms of entertainment and works something like this: former F1 suppliers Dallara [chassis] and Judd [engines] are putting together a batch of identical 700bhp single-seaters, which will be turned out in the colours of Europe's leading soccer clubs and driven by a mixture of rising and established stars.

The concept was received with mixed reactions – and from within the establishment they were largely negative. McLaren head honcho Ron Dennis said: "I think a football team full of grand prix drivers would attract more support than a field full of grand prix look-alikes in soccer colours. As an alternative to F1, it's hardly worth talking about."

FIA president Max Mosley added: "They are perfectly welcome to have a go, but if we went and named football clubs after F1 teams, I'm not sure people would pay to watch."

P1GP remained adamant, however, about the validity of its concept. Spokesman Gary Crumpler, formerly of Williams, said: "People love motor racing, but in most countries they only get one chance a year to see a truly top-class event. There is room for competition in all walks of life – McDonald's has Burger King and Coca-Cola has Pepsi, so why shouldn't there be a rival to F1?"

Rarer than a decent England left-back: Frentzen (above left) actually finished.

IT WAS A RELIEF FOR HEINZ-HARALD FRENTZEN TO MAKE THE FINISH FOR ONCE AND THE JORDAN DRIVER CLAIMED THE FINAL POINT

He might have been up and down in qualifying as he tried myriad different set-ups, but in the race he was absolutely consistent.

Early on, when he pushed to make a break, he was revving his Ilmor-Mercedes V10 a little harder than usual, which sent worrying messages to McLaren's pit wall telemetry, but he cooled his tactics just as the team was about to order him to do so.

His faultless afternoon's work earned him a two-point championship lead – the first time anyone other than Schuey had led this year – and put McLaren ahead of Ferrari in the constructors' battle, too.

Resigned to his fate, Schumacher settled for making sure he stayed ahead of the other McLaren. Coulthard struggled in the opening third of the race, because his chassis felt unbalanced for the first time all weekend. The rear tyres from that stint were found to be running slightly higher than ideal pressures, however, and thereafter he sped up and caught Schumacher. He might even have put the German under serious pressure had his pursuit not been hindered, at various stages, by both Minardis [see sidebar].

Ralf Schumacher made a great start and momentarily passed Coulthard, but the Williams-BMW driver eventually had to settle for fifth because a jammed wheel nut slowed his first stop and dropped him behind Rubens Barrichello's off-the-pace Ferrari.

It was a relief for Heinz-Harald Frentzen to make the finish for once and the Jordan driver claimed the final point – which Jenson Button had been chasing until his engine began to misbehave in the closing stages.

As hordes of tired, drunken fans began to leave, or else took refuge in the licensed brothel/camping facility that had thoughtfully been placed by the circuit entrance, Schuey was looking a touch less chipper than he did after his flying start to the campaign.

"If we continue like this, we have no chance," he said.

STARTING GRID

3 M Schumacher
1m17.514s

2 Coulthard
1m17.886s

1 Hakkinen
1m17.922s

9 R Schumacher
1m18.321s

4 Barrichello
1m18.330s

5 Frentzen
1m18.523s

11 Fisichella
1m18.607s

10 Button
1m18.699s

17 Salo
1m18.748s

7 Irvine
1m19.008s

12 Wurz
1m19.259s

6 Trulli
1m19.266s

16 Diniz
1m19.451s

14 Alesi
1m19.626s

18 de la Rosa
1m19.897s

22 Villeneuve
1m19.937s

8 Herbert
1m19.956s

23 Zonta
1m20.272s

15 Heidfeld
1m20.481s

19 Verstappen
1m20.609s

20 Gené
1m20.654s

21 Mazzacane
1m20.905s

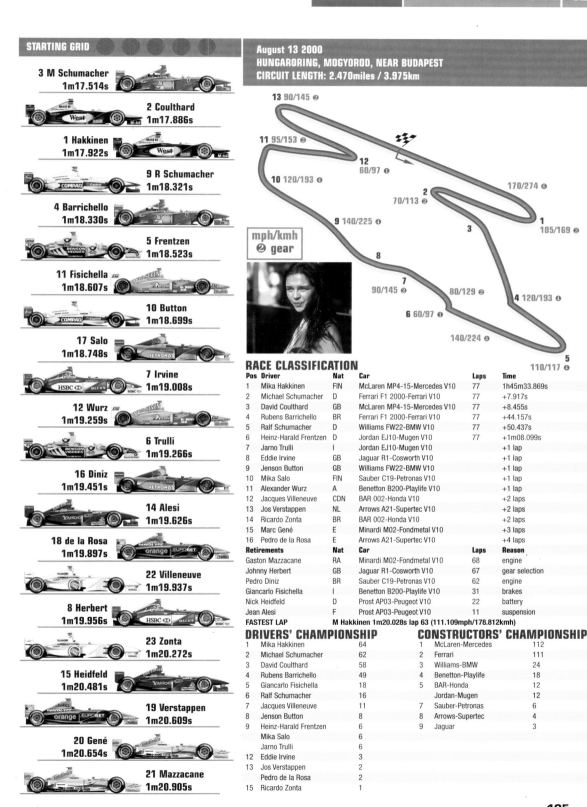

August 13 2000
HUNGARORING, MOGYOROD, NEAR BUDAPEST
CIRCUIT LENGTH: 2.470miles / 3.975km

13 90/145 ❷
11 95/153 ❷
12 60/97 ❶
10 120/193 ❶
2 70/113 ❷
170/274 ❻
9 140/225 ❻
3
1 105/169 ❷
8
7 90/145 ❷
80/129 ❷
4 120/193 ❻
6 60/97 ❶
140/224 ❻
5 110/117 ❶

mph/kmh
❷ gear

RACE CLASSIFICATION

Pos	Driver	Nat	Car	Laps	Time
1	Mika Hakkinen	FIN	McLaren MP4-15-Mercedes V10	77	1h45m33.869s
2	Michael Schumacher	D	Ferrari F1 2000-Ferrari V10	77	+7.917s
3	David Coulthard	GB	McLaren MP4-15-Mercedes V10	77	+8.455s
4	Rubens Barrichello	BR	Ferrari F1 2000-Ferrari V10	77	+44.157s
5	Ralf Schumacher	D	Williams FW22-BMW V10	77	+50.437s
6	Heinz-Harald Frentzen	D	Jordan EJ10-Mugen V10	77	+1m08.099s
7	Jarno Trulli	I	Jordan EJ10-Mugen V10		+1 lap
8	Eddie Irvine	GB	Jaguar R1-Cosworth V10		+1 lap
9	Jenson Button	GB	Williams FW22-BMW V10		+1 lap
10	Mika Salo	FIN	Sauber C19-Petronas V10		+1 lap
11	Alexander Wurz	A	Benetton B200-Playlife V10		+1 lap
12	Jacques Villeneuve	CDN	BAR 002-Honda V10		+2 laps
13	Jos Verstappen	NL	Arrows A21-Supertec V10		+2 laps
14	Ricardo Zonta	BR	BAR 002-Honda V10		+2 laps
15	Marc Gené	E	Minardi M02-Fondmetal V10		+3 laps
16	Pedro de la Rosa	E	Arrows A21-Supertec V10		+4 laps

Retirements	Nat	Car	Laps	Reason
Gaston Mazzacane	RA	Minardi M02-Fondmetal V10	68	engine
Johnny Herbert	GB	Jaguar R1-Cosworth V10	67	gear selection
Pedro Diniz	BR	Sauber C19-Petronas V10	62	engine
Giancarlo Fisichella	I	Benetton B200-Playlife V10	31	brakes
Nick Heidfeld	D	Prost AP03-Peugeot V10	22	battery
Jean Alesi	F	Prost AP03-Peugeot V10	11	suspension

FASTEST LAP M Hakkinen 1m20.028s lap 63 (111.109mph/178.812kmh)

DRIVERS' CHAMPIONSHIP

1	Mika Hakkinen	64
2	Michael Schumacher	62
3	David Coulthard	58
4	Rubens Barrichello	49
5	Giancarlo Fisichella	18
6	Ralf Schumacher	16
7	Jacques Villeneuve	11
8	Jenson Button	8
9	Heinz-Harald Frentzen	6
	Mika Salo	6
	Jarno Trulli	6
12	Eddie Irvine	3
13	Jos Verstappen	2
	Pedro de la Rosa	2
15	Ricardo Zonta	1

CONSTRUCTORS' CHAMPIONSHIP

1	McLaren-Mercedes	112
2	Ferrari	111
3	Williams-BMW	24
4	Benetton-Playlife	18
5	BAR-Honda	12
	Jordan-Mugen	12
7	Sauber-Petronas	6
8	Arrows-Supertec	4
9	Jaguar	3

FOSTER'S BELGIAN GRAND PRIX

A WET SPA. THE
PERFECT OPPORTUNITY
FOR SCHUEY TO RECLAIM
THE CHAMPIONSHIP
LEAD. WELL, PERFECT
IN ALL BUT ONE DETAIL:
MIKA WAS QUICKER. THE
FINN'S BREATHTAKING
LATE PASS GAVE
HIM A SIX-POINT
CHAMPIONSHIP
ADVANTAGE

Jealous guy: as Mika and Michael discuss the art of
200mph dodgems [above], Schuey looks downcast after
spotting his rival's titanium wedding ring, which is
much better than his poncy gold number. Hakkinen
left his memorable pass until late, by which time all
the photographers were waiting by the finishing line.
So here's a shot [left] of him simply being good rather
than great

IN THE IMMEDIATE AFTERMATH, THERE WAS NEAR HYSTERIA. SOME SECTIONS of the press started warbling on about how this had been one of the greatest moments in the history of the sport. Which it wasn't.

They were talking about a manoeuvre on the 41st of 44 laps at a wet-dry Spa-Francorchamps. Dubiously repelled at about 200mph when he tried to take the lead during the previous lap, Mika Hakkinen outfoxed Michael Schumacher as the pair came up behind Ricardo Zonta's about-to-be-lapped BAR.

Approaching Les Combes at the end of the long climb up from Raidillon, Schumacher passed to Zonta's left and set himself up to take a conventional line into the impending corner. Hakkinen, meanwhile, went to the Brazilian's right and carried enough momentum to draw alongside Schuey and edge ahead under braking.

It was a fine, opportunistic and spectacular move by a man who was simply doing what he is paid millions of pounds per annum to do. But it was hardly the pivotal moment in motor sport history it was later portrayed to be.

Straight after the race, Hakkinen and the visibly crestfallen Schuey discussed things privately for a couple of moments. The hand signals were clear: they weren't talking about the pass, but about the lap before, when they had all but collided while travelling flat out. Indeed, their cars bore physical evidence that they had touched. But Hakkinen hadn't felt it and, elated, he wasn't about to get into a post-race slanging match. He preferred to focus on the positives. "On the lap I passed, I knew Michael wouldn't give me room at the end of the straight," he said, "so I took Plan B. I picked up a bit of a slipstream from Zonta, which gave me some extra speed. I just loved that move, really loved it. Not sure that Michael did, though."

It had been a spellbinding end to a compelling race, which started behind the Safety Car on a damp track. Memories of the 12-car pile-up here in soggy 1998 were still too fresh.

Comfortably on pole position ahead of young chargers Jarno Trulli and Jenson Button, and with Ferrari's grumpy old codger

STRAIGHT AFTER THE RACE, HAKKINEN AND THE VISIBLY CRESTFALLEN SCHUEY DISCUSSED THINGS PRIVATELY FOR A COUPLE OF MOMENTS

Demon Hill: Coulthard sweeps to the top of Eau Rouge [main shot], where the McLarens looked fast and balanced all weekend, just as they did on the rest of the circuit. Alesi [top left] was heroic, but his car was typically rubbish. Schuey slices inside Trulli [above right]. Jarno walks away [above left] seconds later after Button had tried, but failed, to mimic the German

KID JENSON

only fourth, Hakkinen sped into an early lead and kept it after stopping for dry tyres on lap seven. It was a later pit call than it should have been, however, and McLaren waited yet another lap to service David Coulthard, whose race was seriously compromised – not for the first time this season.

Prost's Jean Alesi had stopped for slicks on the fourth lap and almost immediately set fastest lap. Everyone apart from McLaren appeared to notice; Hakkinen just got away with it, but his team-mate dropped to ninth.

It wasn't the only thing Hakkinen got away with, because on the 13th lap he spun at Stavelot and handed the lead to Schuey, who had taken second with relative ease by passing Button and Trulli in quick succession at the end of lap four. When Button tried to follow him past the Jordan, the two collided and Trulli was out on the spot [see sidebar].

Given the lead in tricky conditions at Spa, you'd expect Schuey to romp away – but not this time. After the top two had made

Several races in 2000 underlined what Williams was letting slip through its fingers by releasing Jenson Button to Benetton, but Spa was perhaps the most striking example.

The 20-year-old Englishman was looking forward to this one because, along with Silverstone, it was one of only two tracks where he had prior experience. It showed.

His pace in free practice and qualifying rattled team-mate Ralf Schumacher and, as he had in the British GP, he lined up ahead of both Schueys. "I sort of expected to be in the top six because I know the track," he said, "although I never expected to be third. But you are never satisfied in this business. I reckon I could have been a bit faster."

Speed is one thing, race experience at this level quite another. At the end of the fourth lap, while pondering an attack on second-fastest qualifier Jarno Trulli at the Bus Stop chicane [above], Button was momentarily caught off guard and allowed Michael Schumacher to nick past on the inside. The German calmly breezed past Trulli at the next corner, La Source and, thinking this looked like a good idea, Jenson tried to follow. Clump!

The unfortunate Trulli, who had tucked team-mate Heinz-Harald Frentzen up very neatly all weekend, looped round into a spin, got out and stomped away. "Jenson was too aggressive, too soon," he said. "There wasn't room. He should have waited another lap or two.

Commendably, Button put up his hand and apologised. The incident didn't quite ruin his race – but without it he might well have had more than a fifth place to show for his efforts.

United culler of Benettons: Fisichella wrecked a car on Sunday morning (above) and did a bit less damage to the spare in the afternoon

TO MAKE MATTERS WORSE, TRACK MARSHALS PUT FISICHELLA'S CAR ON A CRANE AND PROMPTLY SMACKED IT INTO THE BARRIERS

their single fuel stops the German was five seconds to the good – but Hakkinen was closing, and continued to do so until they came up behind the ambling Zonta when the race reached its thrilling, decisive crux. Zonta, of course, had the best view in the house. "It was," he said, "a fantastic move. Mika came really close to me. I just tried to stay in the centre of the road, out of the way."

Although Button's performance had been the talk of qualifying, it was his team-mate Ralf Schumacher who took third in the race after a smart, controlled drive.

Coulthard recovered to take fourth ahead of Button, whose steering felt heavy following his early clash with Trulli. The final point – for the second straight race – went to Heinz-Harald Frentzen, but there was bitter disappointment for poor Alesi.

His cavalier early tyre stop had helped elevate him to fourth place – and despite being armed only with a Prost he looked as if he might hold it, too, until his fuel system packed up with 12 laps to go.

Even so, he had a better day than Giancarlo Fisichella, who rolled his Benetton at Stavelot during the morning warm-up. In the race his engine died on lap nine, which led to him being rammed by the following Jos Verstappen. To make matters even worse, the track marshals put his car on a crane and promptly smacked it into the barriers.

EVERY LOSER WINS

Jenson Button's continually impressive form wasn't just good news for the Englishman.

In the FIA F3000 Championship paddock, on the other side of the tall security fence that separates F1 from the outside world, Williams test driver Bruno Junqueira [above] was lapping it up, too.

At the start of the year, Junqueira had been the loser in a two-way dogfight for the second Williams seat alongside Ralf Schumacher. For the sake of about one-tenth of a second, the job went Jenson's way. Junqueira would spend the season doing lots of background work for Williams – in his spare time between trying to win the FIA F3000 title.

On Saturday afternoon at Spa, shortly after Button had clinched third spot on the F1 grid, Junqueira took part in the F3000 finale. In the early stages of the race, the Petrobras Lola driver's engine lost power and he slumped from third place to ninth. With sole title rival Nicolas Minassian failing to win, however, the title was Junqueira's.

His post-race smile stretched most of the way to Germany. "Finishing ninth isn't a great way to take a title," he said, "but I feel elated. This has been a good weekend. People know there wasn't much to choose between Jenson and me at the start of the year. When I see how he is performing with Williams, I regard that as an encouragement because I know I could do a similar job."

Vanquished rival Minassian was one of the first to congratulate Bruno. Gracious in defeat, the Frenchman never once complained that he was racing with a leg injury. Mind you, he was a bit embarrassed about that: he had sliced his right knee with a vacuum nozzle while cleaning his road car.

STARTING GRID

1 Hakkinen
1m50.646s

6 Trulli
1m51.419s

10 Button
1m51.444s

3 M Schumacher
1m51.552s

2 Coulthard
1m51.587s

9 R Schumacher
1m51.743s

22 Villeneuve
1m51.799s

5 Frentzen
1m51.926s

8 Herbert
1m52.242s

4 Barrichello
1m52.444s

11 Fisichella
1m52.756s

7 Irvine
1m52.885s

23 Zonta
1m53.002s

15 Heidfeld
1m53.193s

16 Diniz
1m53.211s

18 de la Rosa
1m53.237s

14 Alesi
1m53.309s

17 Salo
1m53.357s

12 Wurz
1m53.403s

19 Verstappen
1m53.912s

20 Gené
1m54.680s

21 Mazzacane
1m54.784s

August 27 2000
CIRCUIT DE SPA-FRANCORCHAMPS, STAVELOT
CIRCUIT LENGTH: 4.33 miles / 6.968km

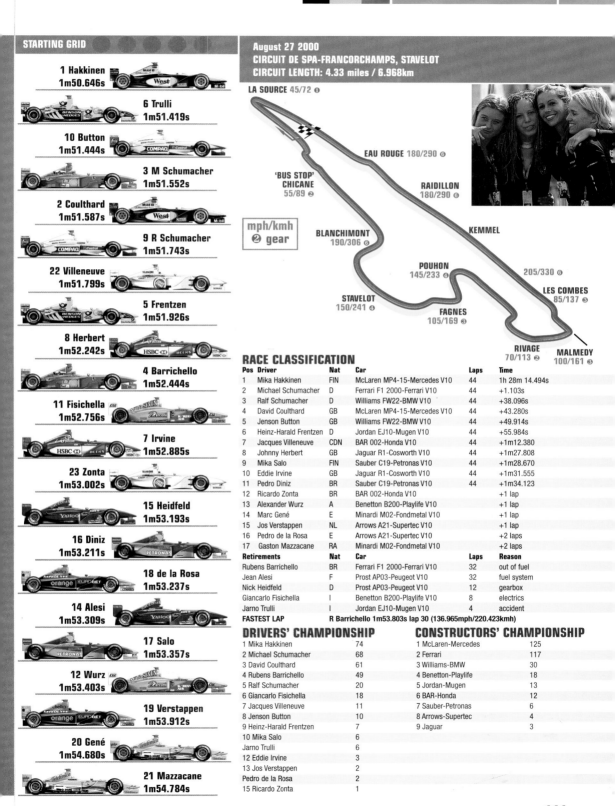

LA SOURCE 45/72 ❶

EAU ROUGE 180/290 ❻

'BUS STOP' CHICANE 55/89 ❷

RAIDILLON 180/290 ❻

BLANCHIMONT 190/306 ❻

KEMMEL

mph/kmh
❷ gear

POUHON 145/233 ❹

205/330 ❻

LES COMBES 85/137 ❸

STAVELOT 150/241 ❹

FAGNES 105/169 ❸

RIVAGE 70/113 ❷

MALMEDY 100/161 ❸

RACE CLASSIFICATION

Pos	Driver	Nat	Car	Laps	Time
1	Mika Hakkinen	FIN	McLaren MP4-15-Mercedes V10	44	1h 28m 14.494s
2	Michael Schumacher	D	Ferrari F1 2000-Ferrari V10	44	+1.103s
3	Ralf Schumacher	D	Williams FW22-BMW V10	44	+38.096s
4	David Coulthard	GB	McLaren MP4-15-Mercedes V10	44	+43.280s
5	Jenson Button	GB	Williams FW22-BMW V10	44	+49.914s
6	Heinz-Harald Frentzen	D	Jordan EJ10-Mugen V10	44	+55.984s
7	Jacques Villeneuve	CDN	BAR 002-Honda V10	44	+1m12.380
8	Johnny Herbert	GB	Jaguar R1-Cosworth V10	44	+1m27.808
9	Mika Salo	FIN	Sauber C19-Petronas V10	44	+1m28.670
10	Eddie Irvine	GB	Jaguar R1-Cosworth V10	44	+1m31.555
11	Pedro Diniz	BR	Sauber C19-Petronas V10	44	+1m34.123
12	Ricardo Zonta	BR	BAR 002-Honda V10		+1 lap
13	Alexander Wurz	A	Benetton B200-Playlife V10		+1 lap
14	Marc Gené	E	Minardi M02-Fondmetal V10		+1 lap
15	Jos Verstappen	NL	Arrows A21-Supertec V10		+1 lap
16	Pedro de la Rosa	E	Arrows A21-Supertec V10		+2 laps
17	Gaston Mazzacane	RA	Minardi M02-Fondmetal V10		+2 laps

Retirements	Nat	Car	Laps	Reason
Rubens Barrichello	BR	Ferrari F1 2000-Ferrari V10	32	out of fuel
Jean Alesi	F	Prost AP03-Peugeot V10	32	fuel system
Nick Heidfeld	D	Prost AP03-Peugeot V10	12	gearbox
Giancarlo Fisichella	I	Benetton B200-Playlife V10	8	electrics
Jarno Trulli	I	Jordan EJ10-Mugen V10	4	accident

FASTEST LAP R Barrichello 1m53.803s lap 30 (136.965mph/220.423kmh)

DRIVERS' CHAMPIONSHIP

1 Mika Hakkinen	74
2 Michael Schumacher	68
3 David Coulthard	61
4 Rubens Barrichello	49
5 Ralf Schumacher	20
6 Giancarlo Fisichella	18
7 Jacques Villeneuve	11
8 Jenson Button	10
9 Heinz-Harald Frentzen	7
10 Mika Salo	6
Jarno Trulli	6
12 Eddie Irvine	3
15 Jos Verstappen	2
Pedro de la Rosa	2
15 Ricardo Zonta	1

CONSTRUCTORS' CHAMPIONSHIP

1 McLaren-Mercedes	125
2 Ferrari	117
3 Williams-BMW	30
4 Benetton-Playlife	18
5 Jordan-Mugen	13
6 BAR-Honda	12
7 Sauber-Petronas	6
8 Arrows-Supertec	4
9 Jaguar	3

NEW KIDS

THE ROAD TO FORMULA ONE IS BECOMING EVER HARDER FOR YOUNG DRIVERS. THE SPORT HAS A LOGICAL LINE OF PROGRESSION, BUT IT CONFUSES THE ISSUE WHEN THE JENSON BUTTONS OF THIS WORLD BULLDOZE THEIR WAY THROUGH. ARE YOU REALLY PAST IT IF AN F1 TEAM HASN'T SIGNED YOU BY YOUR FOURTH BIRTHDAY? HERE ARE A FEW BLOKES WHO HOPE OTHERWISE

FERNANDO ALONSO, E

2000 RECORD: Reigning Formula Nissan champ jumped into FIA F3000 series. In only his second year of car racing, showed predictable blend of speed and impatience until the end of the year [when he just showed speed]. Finished second in Hungary and took his Team Astromega Lola to easy victory at Spa [left], a track he barely knew. Only 19, and poised to be motor racing's greatest-ever Spaniard.
F1 POTENTIAL: 10/10

ON THE TRACK

SÉBASTIEN BOURDAIS, F

2000 RECORD: Came to the FIA F3000 series as reigning French F3 champ. Studious and articulate out of the car; equally fluent on the track. Qualified on front row at Monaco, despite never having been before. Second at Magny-Cours. France is desperate for young talent to help out F1 codger Alesi. Sébastien is handily placed to oblige.
F1 POTENTIAL: 9/10

FERNANDO ALONSO WON EASILY AT SPA. HE'S ONLY 19 – AND POISED TO BE MOTOR RACING'S GREATEST-EVER SPANIARD

ANTONIO PIZZONIA, BR

2000 RECORD: Won the British F3 title, which was largely expected, and also impressed when he drove a 700bhp BriSCA F1 Stock Car for a laugh. Has all the pre-requisites [speed, small and light enough to get in a modern racing car, marketing advantages of being Amazonian, quick name], but also has a slightly suspect temperament in that he doesn't always feel like driving if the car's rubbish.
F1 POTENTIAL: 9/10

ALSO WORTH WATCHING

A few other names that caught our eye during the past season

David Saelens [B], left: but only because he kept driving into people [usually Sébastien Bourdais] during F3000 races. Fast, though. **Damien Faulkner** [GB]: won the Euro Formula Palmer Audi title – the same series that produced the promising Justin Wilson [see page 115]. **Enrique Bernoldi** [BR]: very quick in F3000, but could have done with a car that ran for more than seven minutes at a time.

Giorgio Pantano [I], left: karting hero switched to German F3 with impressive results. **André Lotterer** [B] below left: one of about 15 youngsters on Jaguar's wish-list. Rapid in German F3. **Ricardo Sperafico** [BR]: won Italian domestic F3000 series.

Significance uncertain, but looks good on the CV. **Dan Wheldon** [GB]: making a name for himself in the USA. Second in the high-profile Toyota Atlantic series. **James Courtney** [AUS], below: class of the field in British Formula Ford, which is still a top barometer. **Anthony Davidson** [GB]: triumphed in the Formula Ford Festival, the

world's second-finest event [behind the street-racing festival in Pau, France]. **Jack Straw's chauffeur**: 103mph on the M4.

TOMAS SCHECKTER, ZA

2000 RECORD: Son of 1979 world champion Jody drove in British F3 [second to Pizzonia] and also competed sporadically in FIA F3000 series [one second place, at Hockenheim] and Italian domestic F3000 series [finished second at Monza]. There's no truth in the rumour that he'll combine Jaguar F1 test duties in 2001 with a milk round.

F1 POTENTIAL: 10/10

JONATHAN COCHET, F

2000 RECORD: Won his national F3 title plus blue-riband races at Pau and Zandvoort. Only possible drawback is historical improbability of making it to F1 if you are called Jonathan.

F1 POTENTIAL: 7/10

MARK WEBBER, AUS

2000 RECORD: Almost forgotten after Mercedes abandoned its sports car programme and left him on the sidelines, Webber managed to wriggle out of his contract and re-establish himself as a top-line single-seater crusader with Eurobet Arrows in the FIA F3000 series. Third in the championship – and best rookie. Memorable win at Silverstone. Incredibly level-headed. Will test for Benetton in 2001.

F1 POTENTIAL: 10/10

KIMI RAIKKONEN, FIN

2000 RECORD: Experienced Finnish kartist switched to cars in 1999, won the British Formula Renault Sport title this year and was testing for Sauber by the autumn. As we closed for press, the Swiss team was thought to be on the verge of signing the 21-year-old to partner Nick Heidfeld next year. Makes Jenson Button's progress look slow, frankly. Next thing you know, Ron Dennis and co are going to be hiding round corners in Helsinki, poised to snap them up as they pass their tests.

F1 POTENTIAL: 10/10, APPARENTLY

KIMI RAIKKONEN MAKES JENSON BUTTON'S PROGRESS LOOK SLOW, FRANKLY

WHATEVER HAPPENED TO?

LAST YEAR WE TIPPED 14 DRIVERS FOR THE TOP (BUT WE HAD MORE SPACE ALLOCATED TO THIS FEATURE THAN WE DO NOW). NEXT YEAR FOUR OF THEM WILL BE IN FORMULA ONE AND THREE WILL BE IN THE TOP-LEVEL US-BASED CHAMP CAR SERIES. EIGHT OF THEM COULD BE SAID TO HAVE PROGRESSED, AND ONLY TWO TO HAVE REGRESSED. BY SIGNING FOR PROST, HOWEVER, NICK HEIDFELD MANAGED TO GO FORWARDS BUT BACKWARDS IN ONE MOVE.
HERE'S A BRIEF GUIDE TO THEIR FORTUNES:

POSITIVES

JENSON BUTTON

We gave him an 8/10 chance of making F1. We undersold him. Supersonic

JUAN PABLO MONTOYA

Still the fastest man in Champ Car racing, though his car was frail. Drives a Williams-BMW in F1 next year

BRUNO JUNQUEIRA

Won the FIA F3000 title. Off to race Champ Cars

NICOLAS MINASSIAN

Pipped to the F3000 title by Junqueira. Also off to race Champ Cars

LUCIANO BURTI

Tested for Jaguar. Raced once. Full-time F1 job next year

JUSTIN WILSON

Enhanced reputation as an F3000 front-liner. Stays in the series with Coca-Cola backed Nordic team

DARREN MANNING

Emerged as a potential F3000 race winner. More of the same coming up

PETER DUMBRECK

Landed a well-paid job with Merc, but is Germany's DTM touring car series the way forward?

STATIC

DARIO FRANCHITTI

Tough season, but still a front-runner in Champ Cars. Tested an F1 Jaguar; results inconclusive

MARC HYNES

No money; no drive. 1999 British F3 champ accepted a low-key F3000 deal before stopping to focus on 2001

WESTLEY BARBER

Got a British F3 deal, but things didn't work out. Has time on his side to restore his reputation

FRANCK MONTAGNY

Difficult second season in F3000. Now chasing work in the States. Likely to find some

OOPS

NICK HEIDFELD

Had a great reputation 12 months ago. Then stepped into a Prost. Sauber job in 2001 offers hope of partial salvation

STÉPHANE SARRAZIN

Prost's test driver. Drove for McLaren in F3000. Things didn't go well. Criticised team in the French press, hoping to provoke a few changes. Succeeded. They dropped him

Prancing Horse and market force: fans reveal the
latest replica strip, a Ferrari shirt for darts players
(main shot). Below, Schuey crosses the line to equal
the late Ayrton Senna's tally of 41 GP wins and put
himself joint second in F1's all-time roll of honour

SCHUEY SCORES A
CLASSIC TRIUMPH IN A
RACE TINGED WITH TRAGEDY.
HIS STIRRING PERFORMANCE MIGHT
HAVE REKINDLED HIS TITLE HOPES, BUT
THAT WAS THE LEAST OF HIS – OR F1'S –
CONCERNS AFTER FLYING ACCIDENT DEBRIS
CAUSED THE DEATH OF A MARSHAL

GRAN PREMIO CAMPARI D'ITALIA

A STARK REMINDER

This book seeks to see the lighter side of the sport – and we make no apologies for that. There are days, however, when Formula One has to surrender the obsessions we sometimes mock and take a broader perspective of the world beyond.

Grand prix Sunday at Monza was one such.

Italian fire marshal Paolo Ghislimberti lost his life when he was hit by debris following a pile-up at the second chicane on lap one. The incident started when the Jordans of Heinz-Harald Frentzen and Jarno Trulli came together with Rubens Barrichello's Ferrari, which spun across the track and punted David Coulthard's McLaren out of the race. Moments later, Pedro de la Rosa's Arrows – already tumbling over after contact with Johnny Herbert's Jaguar – somersaulted into the gravel and landed amid the wreckage. As bits of racing car flew in all directions, a loose wheel is believed to have struck Ghislimberti and inflicted unsurvivable head and chest injuries.

A full enquiry was launched and the results will be published in due course; legal processes in Italy can be painfully slow.

Several F1 drivers attended the funeral and all teams made a donation to Ghislimberti's widow.

The drivers involved were lucky – particularly Barrichello, who was struck on the head by de la Rosa's car. This time, the same could not be said for an innocent bystander.

Everyone involved in the sport is aware of the potential dangers – but stark reminders such as this don't make the truth any more palatable.

Jaguar XJ sick: Irvine (background, right) goes off at the first corner as Heidfeld and the Arrows twins pick their way through the fling polystyrene. Unable to attack Schu, Hakkinen settled for monstering the kerbs instead (main sh...

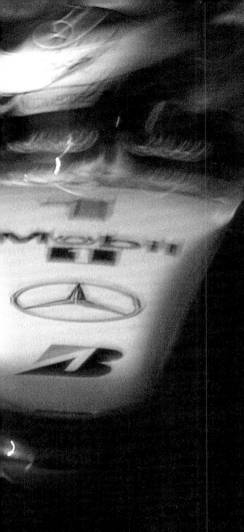

FERRARI RETURNED TO ITS HOME PATCH AFTER FOUR RACES IN WHICH McLAREN had thrashed the pride of Italy. So where would you have placed your bet before this one?

Obvious, of course. Ferrari was not about to chuck in the towel when fierce local pride was at stake. If its once prosperous world title hopes were going to be vanquished, it wasn't going to happen at Monza.

Ferrari was in barnstorming form all weekend. Michael Schumacher and Rubens Barrichello monopolised the front row of the grid and Schuey went on to dominate the race. Traction control might be banned in F1; cruise control patently isn't.

Where did Ferrari find this sudden upturn in form? We'll probably never know. Before the start, Schumacher spoke about top secret "novelties" to be introduced before the end of the season. Post-race, however, he went very quiet about any gimmicks.

Ferrari's corporate line throughout the weekend was that the team had failed to get its car working properly for any of the five previous races. Ferrari technical director Ross Brawn said: "The car has been capable of going a lot quicker than it has of late, but since Magny-Cours we've had tyre problems. We have worked hard to overcome this and things have been good here. At Spa we were a second off the pace in qualifying, but that was because we never managed a clear lap. Now, we're back to where we should be."

Mika Hakkinen didn't need to be told as much. Immediately after qualifying third behind the red army, the Finn went to have a good look at the back of the Ferrari. The chances of him noticing anything new on the car were slight, but his body language was clear: he didn't think the Ferrari should have been that fast.

"It's always interesting to look at our competitors' cars," Hakkinen said.. "Just a curiosity. You don't necessarily learn anything."

McLaren boss Ron Dennis was not unduly concerned at his nemesis's sudden surge of form and said he expected a different story in the race. When that failed to materialise, he remained calm and succinct.

He said: "This is a circuit that doesn't really play to the aerodynamic strengths we have. This is not sour grapes – we think we would have had a very good chance if we had been able to balance our car."

At least Hakkinen went away with second place in his pocket on a day of rare attrition. Many cars failed even to last beyond the first lap. Before the race, prophets of doom had forecast that the redesigned first chicane would catch people out, but only former Ferrari team-mates Eddie Irvine and Mika Salo tripped and stumbled over each other. It was at the second chicane that the main drama occurred, when a multi-car accident led to debris flying over the barriers and, sadly, inflicting fatal injuries to a marshal [see sidebar].

Whatever happened after that would be of secondary significance. In the immediate aftermath, the field – reduced by seven - trudged around behind the Safety Car for 10 laps while the crash situation was dealt with.

Just before the Safety Car finally peeled in, Schuey slowed

MIKA'S BODY LANGUAGE WAS CLEAR: HE DIDN'T THINK THE FERRARI SHOULD HAVE BEEN THAT FAST

AN EXHIBITION OF HEART

When Michael Schumacher [above] broke down in tears after the Italian Grand Prix, it was widely reported as being the first known instance of a robot making his feelings known in public.

That, however, rather misses the point. Schuey is traditionally emotional in the wake of race wins – it's just that his gestures are usually more overtly buoyant and positive.

He broke down when an interviewer reminded him that he had equalled the late Ayrton Senna's career total of 41 grand prix victories. Several of F1's most chaotic minutes of live TV followed while Schuey blubbed, the perplexed Mika Hakkinen refused to answer questions and Schuey Jnr did his best to string a sentence together while trying to console his brother.

There was an unlikely source of compassion in the form of McLaren boss Ron Dennis, who said: "I don't know what part of the interview got to him, but it certainly got to him. But I'm not surprised. It's very, very hard to succeed in this sport and, when you have success, sometimes the adrenalin isn't there any more and emotion floods over you."

Later, the German would only say that his tears came after a weekend of pure struggle that had been intensified by the overwhelming support of the local fans.

The next day *Bild*, Germany's answer to *The Sun*, ran the headline: "You are not a cold racing machine, Schumi. We've seen your heart!" Their subject, back to his usual form, was unmoved. He said: "What I have heard is that people suddenly see me as a human, which I rather struggle with. I always thought I was human before."

Points makes surprises, clockwise from top left: Zonta and Verstappen starred; Wurz – no, we don't know what came over him, either; the non-blubbing Schuey was third

BEHIND THE LEADERS, JOS VERSTAPPEN AND RICARDO ZONTA PUT IN SUPERB PERFORMANCES, CHARGING THROUGH THE FIELD EARLY ON

suddenly to heat up his brakes and Jenson Button – running at the back of the lead group – was caught unawares. He swerved off the track to avoid running into Jacques Villeneuve's BAR just ahead.

Villeneuve thought Button should have been watching more carefully but, uncharacteristically, Schumacher apologised for causing the problem. "What I did was normal," he said, "but the way I did it was a mistake. I'm sorry for whoever suffered from that – I thought everybody would know what I was going to do, but further back many cars struggle to see."

Once the race resumed the German pulled away by half a second per lap for the next 20 laps. Ferrari and McLaren carried out immaculate pit stops, but Schumacher had done enough. Some way back, sibling Ralf joined the top two on the podium.

Behind the leaders, Jos Verstappen and Ricardo Zonta put in superb performances, charging through the field early on before taking fourth and sixth, either side of surprise points-scorer Alexander Wurz.

The post-race press conference took place before the consequences of the opening-lap accident had been made public – and Schuey's tears showed how much this win had meant. In his words, Ferrari was "back on the road".

STARTING GRID

3 M Schumacher
1m23.770s

4 Barrichello
1m23.797s

1 Hakkinen
1m23.967s

22 Villeneuve
1m24.238s

2 Coulthard
1m24.290s

6 Trulli
1m 24.477s

9 R Schumacher
1m24.516s

5 Frentzen
1m24.766s

11 Fisichella
1m24.789s

18 de la Rosa
1m24.814s

19 Verstappen
1m24.820s

10 Button
1m24.907s

12 Wurz
1m25.150s

7 Irvine
1m25.251s

17 Salo
1m25.322s

16 Diniz
1m25.324s

23 Zonta
1m25.337s

8 Herbert
1m25.388s

14 Alesi
1m25.556s

15 Heidfeld
1m25.625s

20 Gené
1m26.336s

21 Mazzacane
1m27.360s

September 10 2000
AUTODROMO NAZIONALE DI MONZA, NEAR MILAN
CIRCUIT LENGTH: 3.585miles / 5.770km

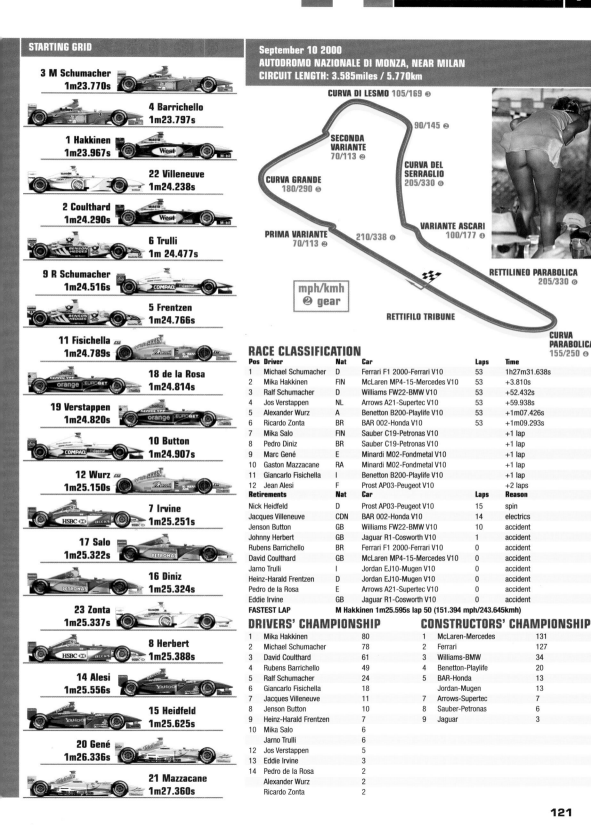

CURVA DI LESMO 105/169 ③

90/145 ②

SECONDA VARIANTE 70/113 ②

CURVA DEL SERRAGLIO 205/330 ⑥

CURVA GRANDE 180/290 ⑤

VARIANTE ASCARI 100/177 ④

PRIMA VARIANTE 70/113 ②

210/338 ⑥

RETTILINEO PARABOLICA 205/330 ⑥

mph/kmh ② gear

RETTIFILO TRIBUNE

CURVA PARABOLICA 155/250 ④

RACE CLASSIFICATION

Pos	Driver	Nat	Car	Laps	Time
1	Michael Schumacher	D	Ferrari F1 2000-Ferrari V10	53	1h27m31.638s
2	Mika Hakkinen	FIN	McLaren MP4-15-Mercedes V10	53	+3.810s
3	Ralf Schumacher	D	Williams FW22-BMW V10	53	+52.432s
4	Jos Verstappen	NL	Arrows A21-Supertec V10	53	+59.938s
5	Alexander Wurz	A	Benetton B200-Playlife V10	53	+1m07.426s
6	Ricardo Zonta	BR	BAR 002-Honda V10	53	+1m09.293s
7	Mika Salo	FIN	Sauber C19-Petronas V10		+1 lap
8	Pedro Diniz	BR	Sauber C19-Petronas V10		+1 lap
9	Marc Gené	E	Minardi M02-Fondmetal V10		+1 lap
10	Gaston Mazzacane	RA	Minardi M02-Fondmetal V10		+1 lap
11	Giancarlo Fisichella	I	Benetton B200-Playlife V10		+1 lap
12	Jean Alesi	F	Prost AP03-Peugeot V10		+2 laps

Retirements	Nat	Car	Laps	Reason
Nick Heidfeld	D	Prost AP03-Peugeot V10	15	spin
Jacques Villeneuve	CDN	BAR 002-Honda V10	14	electrics
Jenson Button	GB	Williams FW22-BMW V10	10	accident
Johnny Herbert	GB	Jaguar R1-Cosworth V10	1	accident
Rubens Barrichello	BR	Ferrari F1 2000-Ferrari V10	0	accident
David Coulthard	GB	McLaren MP4-15-Mercedes V10	0	accident
Jarno Trulli	I	Jordan EJ10-Mugen V10	0	accident
Heinz-Harald Frentzen	D	Jordan EJ10-Mugen V10	0	accident
Pedro de la Rosa	E	Arrows A21-Supertec V10	0	accident
Eddie Irvine	GB	Jaguar R1-Cosworth V10	0	accident

FASTEST LAP M Hakkinen 1m25.595s lap 50 (151.394 mph/243.645kmh)

DRIVERS' CHAMPIONSHIP

1	Mika Hakkinen	80
2	Michael Schumacher	78
3	David Coulthard	61
4	Rubens Barrichello	49
5	Ralf Schumacher	24
6	Giancarlo Fisichella	18
7	Jacques Villeneuve	11
8	Jenson Button	10
9	Heinz-Harald Frentzen	7
10	Mika Salo	6
	Jarno Trulli	6
12	Jos Verstappen	5
13	Eddie Irvine	3
14	Pedro de la Rosa	2
	Alexander Wurz	2
	Ricardo Zonta	2

CONSTRUCTORS' CHAMPIONSHIP

1	McLaren-Mercedes	131
2	Ferrari	127
3	Williams-BMW	34
4	Benetton-Playlife	20
5	BAR-Honda	13
	Jordan-Mugen	13
7	Arrows-Supertec	7
8	Sauber-Petronas	6
9	Jaguar	3

SAP UNITED STATES GRAND PRIX

LAST TIME FORMULA ONE CAME TO AMERICA, MICHAEL SCHUMACHER WAS STILL RACING SPORTS CARS IN FRONT OF THREE MEN AND A DOG IN HIS FIRST US GP, HE WAS SO FAR AHEAD HE HAD TIME TO MAKE A BEGINNER'S MISTAKE AND STILL WIN WITHOUT BREAKING SWEAT

Crowdburst: the stands are packed solid as the field sets off several seconds after David Coulthard. Note that Brazilians obviously didn't build the scoring tower, because it never fell onto the track at any stage during the weekend

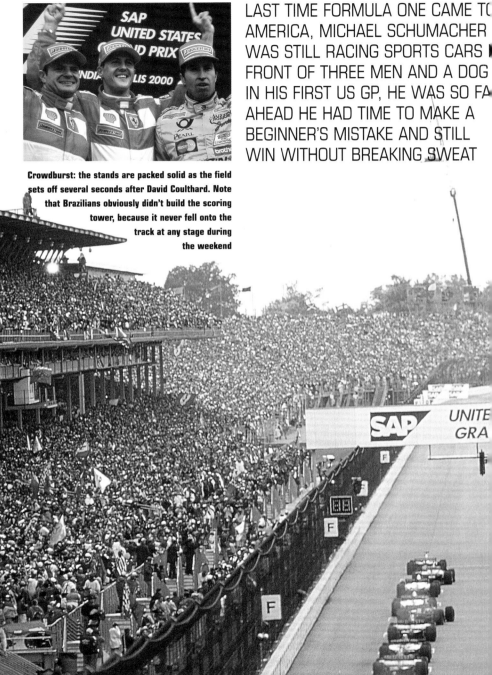

THE FIRST UNITED STATES GRAND PRIX FOR NINE YEARS DIDN'T EXACTLY
produce the three-abreast racing locals have grown accustomed
to with their home-spun motor sports. There were no constant
lead battles and cheerleaders were conspicuous by their absence.

Before a crowd of more than 220,000 – a grand prix record –
Michael Schumacher scored an easy win at Indianapolis to claim
a clear points advantage as the world championship entered its
final phase. With Mika Hakkinen's McLaren retiring in a blaze of
blown Mercedes, Ferrari's first world title for 21 years looked a
real probability for the first time in several weeks.

The German's weekend got off to a flying start when his team
drew on its reserves of strategic invention during the qualifying
hour. The circuit, built within the confines [and using a section]
of Indy's famous oval, incorporated a long, flat out blast during
which cars were on full throttle for about 24 seconds. The
craftiest team in the pit lane sent its two cars out together so that
Schumacher could tuck in behind Rubens Barrichello and profit
from his slipstream before drafting past with a couple of extra
mph under his belt. It gave Schuey a pole-winning edge.

By the time McLaren had worked out what Ferrari was up to,
Hakkinen had used up his full allocation of flying laps, although
he was able to go out to give team-mate David Coulthard a helping
tow, which put the Scot on the front row
at the title-chasing Finn's expense.

Except that the front row would really
be the second row, because Ferrari
sporting director Jean Todt persuaded the
authorities to move pole position back a
few metres. He thought the yard of bricks
that marks Indy's startline – a throwback
that serves as a reminder of the circuit's original paved surface –
might cause Schuey too much wheelspin.

That is never a problem at the track's annual 500-mile or
NASCAR Winston Cup races, both of which feature rolling starts.
And, apparently a stickler for tradition, Coulthard was moving
long before the signal was given and thus established a comfortable
lead while the rest of the field thought about moving off.

Realising that he would be called in for a stop-go penalty within
a few laps, the Scot set about delaying Schumacher to allow
third-placed Hakkinen to close up, exactly the tactic the German
had used so effectively in Malaysia the previous year, when he
blocked the Finn to allow his own team-mate of the time, Eddie
Irvine, to pull away. After seven laps, however, Schumacher
swept by into the first turn. Later, he revealed his powers of
memory retention are less abundant than his driving skills.

"I went really wide to make sure David could not touch me,
but he made it hard to avoid," Schuey said. "I want to make sure
that we don't see team-mates helping drivers fighting for the
championship in a way that is not appropriate."

Coulthard, quite rightly, retorted that you don't have to be in
the championship battle to fight for the race and McLaren boss
Ron Dennis blamed Ferrari for any perceived decline in F1's levels
of sportsmanship.

FERRARI SPORTING DIRECTOR JEAN TODT PERSUADED THE AUTHORITIES TO MOVE POLE POSITION BACK A FEW METRES

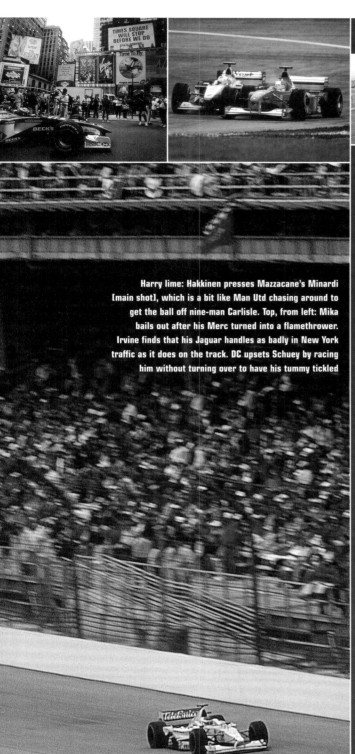

Harry lime: Hakkinen presses Mazzacane's Minardi [main shot], which is a bit like Man Utd chasing around to get the ball off nine-man Carlisle. Top, from left: Mika bails out after his Merc turned into a flamethrower. Irvine finds that his Jaguar handles as badly in New York traffic as it does on the track. DC upsets Schuey by racing him without turning over to have his tummy tickled

DISUNITED STATES

Formula One in America? Rather like luge tobogganing in the Congo or sumo wrestling in Wales, it has never quite caught on.

A 20-year period at Watkins Glen apart, grand prix racing has not had a permanent home in the States. In the relatively recent past it has followed a hobo-like trail from Long Beach to Detroit, a Las Vegas car park, Dallas and Phoenix without ever settling. After the last Phoenix flop in 1991, it vanished altogether.

But Indianapolis promises to be different. By daring to barge in on the venue that Americans, quaintly, consider to be the home of world motor racing, Formula One set itself up for a possible stumble that might lead to its banishment forever from the nation. If it doesn't work at an institution as famous as Indy, they figured, it didn't have a cat in hell's chance anywhere.

The initial prognosis, however, was promising. Fans came, saw, ate hot dogs, got wet and went away with a few more ideas about F1 than they might have had before. Even with the grandstands only half full [the other half didn't overlook the track], the crowd was F1's biggest ever.

Cautiously, the event was regarded as a success – although there remains a little bit of work to do before the its long-term future can be guaranteed.

Doubts remain, for instance, about how many Americans noticed the race outside the Indianapolis Motor Speedway's perimeter walls. It was not televised on any of the three major networks and clashed with a full American football schedule as well as a NASCAR Winston Cup race in Dover, Delaware. NASCAR drivers are household names in the States; F1 racers aren't.

Some traditionalists, meanwhile, had a few biting points to make. Respected *Indianapolis Star* columnist Robin Miller said: "An international treasure has been disfigured to accommodate a group that demands everything but has no loyalty except to the almighty dollar. F1 wouldn't turn Spa into an oval or make Monaco wider, would it?"

COULTHARD RIGHTLY RETORTED THAT YOU DON'T HAVE TO BE IN THE CHAMPIONSHIP BATTLE TO FIGHT

"Ferrari has determined the rules and standards by which we race," he said. "The way they have conducted themselves over the course of the last two years has set the precedent."

With the track still moist after a morning shower, almost everyone started on wet tyres, but it didn't take long before drivers began to peel in for a change. Some stayed out longer than others – and those that did made the right call. One, predictably, was Schumacher, who opened up a handsome lead over Hakkinen [albeit partly aided by an unlikely ally in the form of Gaston Mazzacane, see sidebar].

Once he finally passed the Minardi, Hakkinen set about pursuing his championship rival. Once both were running on dry-weather tyres Hakkinen closed in fast and had reduced the gap to four seconds when his Mercedes cried enough and burst into flames. His demise wiped out any chance of a decent battle for the lead. Schuey added a little spice to the contest by spinning with four laps to go when he momentarily lost concentration, but he was so far ahead by then that he could afford it.

Rubens Barrichello completed Ferrari's delight with a fairly anonymous run to second place, but things weren't so calm further back.

Jenson Button and Jarno Trulli had their second coming-together in the space of three races while battling for fifth on lap two, which led Trulli to criticise the Englishman.

In the closing stages, Jacques Villeneuve's terminal optimism enlivened the contest. The Canadian, winner of the Indy 500 in 1995, tried everything he knew to wrest third place from Heinz-Harald Frentzen. This included not bothering to brake much for the first corner, which worked in as much as he edged ahead of the German, but only for a couple of seconds before he speared across the grass and left himself the task of doing it all again. He was back on Frentzen's tail before the end, but the Jordan driver held on to record only his second podium finish of the season.

Coulthard eventually came in fifth, having not been quite as fast for the rest of the afternoon as he had been at the start.

SMALL FRY FLY

It might not have lasted for the whole race, nor did it have any significant impact on the outcome of the world championship, but for five laps Indianapolis revelled in the spectacle of two McLarens being held up in separate, legitimate racing battles by two Minardis.

What goes around comes around. Towards the end of a season packed with adverse post-race moments by Mika and David about Gaston and Marc, and during which Ron Dennis had hit out at the Italian minnows, Minardi briefly, gloriously turned the tables.

With ten laps gone, Mazzacane held an unprecedented fourth place by dint of not having stopped for dry tyres. But armed only with a three-year-old Ford engine, wets and, well, a Minardi, he kept Mika Hakkinen back for lap after lap [above]. The world champion, who eventually advanced when the Argentine finally pitted for dry tyres, said: "I lost six or seven seconds behind Mazzacane, but I couldn't do anything."

At the same time, Marc Gené comfortably kept Coulthard, who had stopped twice because of his jump-start penalty, back in 15th for six laps.

Team founder Gian Carlo Minardi refused to gloat. He said: "It was satisfying being fourth, but it didn't interest me whether it was Hakkinen behind. Still, both McLarens had a lot of trouble passing us, which means that we were competitive – especially given that we have 100bhp less than them."

Things deteriorated later, however. Both Minardi men overshot their pit bay when they made the second scheduled stops and Mazzacane knocked over a couple of mechanics, fortunately without serious consequences.

Frentzen neighbours, top left: Jordan's sole survivor chased – and beat – the sometimes comedic Jacques Villeneuve to score only his second podium finish of the season

STARTING GRID

3 M Schumacher
1m14.266s

2 Coulthard
1m14.392s

1 Hakkinen
1m14.428s

4 Barrichello
1m14.600s

6 Trulli
1m15.006s

10 Button
1m15.017s

5 Frentzen
1m15.067s

22 Villeneuve
1m15.317s

16 Diniz
1m15.418s

9 R Schumacher
1m15.484s

12 Wurz
1m15.762s

23 Zonta
1m15.784s

19 Verstappen
1m15.808s

17 Salo
1m15.881s

11 Fisichella
1m15.907s

15 Heidfeld
1m16.060s

7 Irvine
1m16.098s

18 de la Rosa
1m16.143s

8 Herbert
1m16.225s

14 Alesi
1m16.471s

21 Mazzacane
1m16.809s

20 Gené
1m17.161s

September 24 2000
INDIANAPOLIS MOTOR SPEEDWAY, INDIANA
CIRCUIT LENGTH: 2.605miles / 4.192km

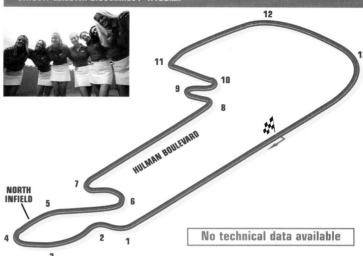

HULMAN BOULEVARD

NORTH INFIELD

No technical data available

RACE CLASSIFICATION

Pos	Driver	Nat	Car	Laps	Time
1	Michael Schumacher	D	Ferrari F1 2000-Ferrari V10	73	1h36m30.883s
2	Rubens Barrichello	BR	Ferrari F1 2000-Ferrari V10	73	+12.118s
3	Heinz-Harald Frentzen	D	Jordan EJ10-Mugen V10	73	+17.368s
4	Jacques Villeneuve	CDN	BAR 002-Honda V10	73	+17.935s
5	David Coulthard	GB	McLaren MP4/15-Mercedes V10	73	+28.813s
6	Ricardo Zonta	BR	BAR 002-Honda V10	73	+51.694s
7	Eddie Irvine	GB	Jaguar R1-Cosworth V10	73	+1m11.115s
8	Pedro Diniz	BR	Sauber C19-Petronas V10		+1 lap
9	Nick Heidfeld	D	Prost AP03-Peugeot V10		+1 lap
10	Alexander Wurz	A	Benetton B200-Playlife V10		+1 lap
11	Johnny Herbert	GB	Jaguar R1-Cosworth V10		+1 lap
12	Marc Gené	E	Minardi M02-Fondmetal V10		+1 lap

Retirements	Nat	Car	Laps	Reason
Jean Alesi	F	Prost AP03-Peugeot V10	64	engine/spin
Gaston Mazzacane	RA	Minardi M02-Fondmetal V10	59	engine
Ralf Schumacher	D	Williams FW22-BMW V10	58	engine hydraulics
Pedro de la Rosa	E	Arrows A21-Supertec V10	45	gearbox
Giancarlo Fisichella	I	Benetton B200-Playlife V10	44	engine
Jos Verstappen	NL	Arrows A21-Supertec V10	34	brakes/accident
Mika Hakkinen	FIN	McLaren MP4/15-Mercedes V10	25	engine
Mika Salo	FIN	Sauber C19-Petronas V10	18	spin
Jenson Button	GB	Williams FW22-BMW V10	14	engine
Jarno Trulli	I	Jordan EJ10-Mugen V10	12	driveshaft

FASTEST LAP D Coulthard 1m14.711s lap 40(125.513mph/201.994kmh)

DRIVERS' CHAMPIONSHIP

1	Michael Schumacher	88
2	Mika Hakkinen	80
3	David Coulthard	63
4	Rubens Barrichello	55
5	Ralf Schumacher	24
6	Giancarlo Fisichella	18
7	Jacques Villeneuve	14
8	Heinz-Harald Frentzen	11
9	Jenson Button	10
10	Mika Salo	6
	Jarno Trulli	6
12	Jos Verstappen	5
13	Eddie Irvine	3
	Ricardo Zonta	3
15	Pedro de la Rosa	2
	Alexander Wurz	2

CONSTRUCTORS' CHAMPIONSHIP

1	Ferrari	143
2	McLaren-Mercedes	133
3	Williams-BMW	34
4	Benetton-Playlife	20
5	BAR-Honda	17
	Jordan-Mugen	17
7	Arrows-Supertec	7
8	Sauber-Petronas	6
9	Jaguar	3

FUJI TELEVISION JAPANESE GRAND PRIX

THE TRACK ALLEGEDLY
FAVOURED McLAREN,
BUT SCHUEY AND FERRARI
GOT THEIR SUMS RIGHT TO
END A 21-YEAR DROUGHT
[AND SETTLE THE TITLE
BEFORE THE FINAL RACE FOR
THE FIRST TIME SINCE 1995]

Fairground attraction: Schuey [left] steams towards
the 43rd win and third world championship title of
his career. Above, Mr and Mrs Schuey react to the
prospect of a pay rise in 2001. If only you knew how
hard it was struggling along on a basic wage of about
£350,000 per week

THERE MIGHT HAVE BEEN 22 DRIVERS ON THE GRID AT SUZUKA, BUT ONLY TWO made any significant contribution to the season's penultimate – and decisive – race.

Immersed in their own private duel, Michael Schumacher and Mika Hakkinen came to Japan with a sharp eye on each other – and but for lapped traffic they could have gone away again without knowing anyone else had been in the fray, such was their dominance.

Not since Schumacher's title win for Benetton in 1995 had the destiny of the championship been decided before the final race of the year – and the German knew victory in Japan would bring him a third world crown. After the agony of being pipped at the final hurdle in 1997 and 1998, he was above averagely determined not to risk having to go through all that again.

The top two's thrilling head-to-head began in qualifying, when Schuey clinched a topsy-turvy pole battle for the sake of 0.009 seconds.

There was nothing to choose between them then – and the same was true of the race. For the third consecutive year in Japan, Hakkinen started on the outside of the front row, the dirtier side of the track. That hadn't stopped the Finn making a flying start in the past, however, and nor did it now. As soon as the start lights flickered off, the McLaren zipped in front and Schumacher's customarily aggressive chop – he appeared to think a right-hand bend had been installed on the grid overnight – provided no defence against the thrusting Finn.

Hakkinen said: "I had to go for it. Michael saw me and knew he did not have a chance, so he let me go."

Schuey was never going to let him get very far, however. The top two might have left the rest of the field trailing, but Mika simply couldn't shake off his immediate pursuer. Prior to the first scheduled refuelling the margin between them never exceeded 2.6 seconds. The stop was critical. Hakkinen came in on lap 22 and Schumacher followed next time around.

Ferrari technical director Ross Brawn said: "We stayed out one lap extra – and by that stage we had seen McLaren's stop and had the benefit of knowing how much fuel Hakkinen had put in. We gave Michael a little bit more so that he could run a slightly longer second stint. The really critical part was making sure Michael held on to Mika in the next sector of the race."

Sure enough, the leaders' pace never abated as they lapped more than a second faster than distant team-mates David Coulthard and Rubens Barrichello. The only glitch came when Schumacher misjudged a passing move as he lapped Ricardo Zonta's BAR. The cars touched slightly, but there was no lasting damage.

By the time the second refuelling stops were due, the track had been made greasy by light drizzle. When Hakkinen peeled in, Schumacher upped his pace for a couple of laps and, when the German stopped two laps later, he needed slightly less fuel

> ## "WE STAYED OUT ONE LAP EXTRA – AND HAD THE BENEFIT OF KNOWING HOW MUCH FUEL HAKKINEN HAD PUT IN"
> ### ROSS BRAWN

Big in Japan: Hakkinen kept his title hopes alive for a while by making the best start [above right] and keeping Schuey contained [right]. Doing it for two-thirds of the race was no use, however. Top, Herbert locks up. Above, Villeneuve practises being Gaston Mazzacane

PEDIGREE CHUMS

Whatever happened to the days when championship rivals hated each other?

Title fighters used to be as quick with their verbal lashings as they were on the track. But not in 2000.

Hakkinen congratulated Schumacher warmly on his championship success [above] – and the German responded by describing Mika as the best rival he had ever faced, thereby managing to be nice while having a simultaneous swipe at former foes Damon Hill and Jacques Villeneuve.

"Mika is a really good guy," Schumacher said. "And you see that particularly in moments when someone loses – although it is wrong to say you are a loser if you come second in this game. The way he reacted was outstanding.

"I have seen many other drivers who have been completely different, trying to make things bad. But Mika is a very positive man who doesn't lose his focus. So he is the best man I have fought for the championship. I hope we have some more good years together."

Not to be outdone in the niceness stakes, Hakkinen retorted: "To be a good winner, sometimes you have to be a good loser, too. I had a great race with Michael and that's what the sport should be all about.

"It would be so wrong for me to say that this was a catastrophe. I don't want to do that. It would be unfair on the sport – and on Michael. I want him to enjoy this day. This is his year. Perhaps next year it will be my turn again. There are plenty more races left in me yet."

On the Button: Jenson [above] was in sparkling form. Right, Ron Dennis ponders playing field flatness. He later apologised for suggesting F1 wasn't fair

THE ONLY OTHER DRIVER TO EMERGE WITH REAL CREDIT WAS JENSON BUTTON, WHO FINISHED FIFTH BEHIND COULTHARD

than his rival to make the end of the race. McLaren's Ron Dennis said: "I don't think our strategy was wrong, but Michael did very quick in and out laps either side of his pit stop."

Schumacher narrowly missed Alexander Wurz's spinning Benetton as he came in for his final helping of fuel and tyres. Later, he described the radio commentary Brawn had given him as he trundled down the pit lane at 50mph to rejoin the race, not knowing quite where Hakkinen was on the other side of the pit wall.

"Ross was saying, 'It's looking good, it's looking good'," Schuey recalled. "I was waiting for him to tell me that it was not good enough, then he said, 'It's looking bloody good'. It was an amazing moment – the best of my career."

When Schuey finally roared out of the pits at full racing speed, Hakkinen was four seconds in arrears and that gap stayed pretty static until the final lap, when the Finn closed up as Schuey eased off. But things were beyond the Finn's control by then.

The long wait was over – five years for Schumacher, 21 for Ferrari.

Brawn said: "As Michael crossed the line, we were speechless. This is the ultimate – exactly what I came to Ferrari for. We've come so close in the last three years – and that makes this win very special."

Hakkinen was magnanimous in defeat – and at least one of his wishes had come true. He said: "I'm relieved that for the first time in three years I can go to the last race knowing I don't have to fight for points."

The top two apart, the only driver to emerge with real credit was Jenson Button, who finished fifth behind Coulthard and Barrichello on his first appearance at one of the championship's most challenging venues.

HI HO SILVER PINING

For Michael Schumacher and Ferrari, the Japanese Grand Prix brought merciful release after five years of torment sprinkled with near misses.

For grand prix racing's armada of conspiracy theorists, events leading up to – and during – the weekend were ripe with tantalising hints of subterfuge.

There are those who allege McLaren is racing against the FIA, as well as 10 other teams. The governing body, however, has always denied outright any allegations of bias towards Ferrari.

There was a whiff of scandal in the air, however, when the FIA suddenly opted to bar teams from using their second cars tactically to delay a potential rival – the very ploy Michael Schumacher had used so effectively to assist Ferrari team-mate Eddie Irvine in the 1999 Malaysian GP. No clear-cut definition about what constituted "delaying tactics" was given, nor was there an explanation of why the new regulation was brought in with two races remaining. Barring exceptional circumstances, rule changes are usually implemented between seasons, not between events.

With Ferrari in the driving seat, McLaren had more need to play tactical games. Williams technical director Patrick Head smiled and said: "Whether it has just occurred to the FIA or whether it is because of special circumstances, I wouldn't like to say."

There were other factors to consider, too. Tyre supplier Bridgestone brought only one rubber compound to a race for the first time – and left behind the soft option that has traditionally suited the McLarens. Oh, and one of the FIA stewards was a lawyer who had successfully argued for Ferrari's reinstatement after its double exclusion from the 1999 Malaysian GP.

One team director said: "Is this a flat playing field? I don't think so." Clue: his cars are predominantly silver.

STARTING GRID

3 M Schumacher
1m35.825s

1 Hakkinen
1m35.834s

2 Coulthard
1m36.236s

4 Barrichello
1m36.330s

10 Button
1m36.628s

9 R Schumacher
1m36.788s

7 Irvine
1m36.899s

5 Frentzen
1m37.243s

22 Villeneuve
1m 37.267s

8 Herbert
1m37.329s

12 Wurz
1m37.348s

11 Fisichella
1m37.479s

18 de la Rosa
1m37.652s

19 Verstappen
1m37.674s

6 Trulli
1m37.679s

15 Heidfeld
1m38.141s

14 Alesi
1m38.209s

23 Zonta
1m38.269s

17 Salo
1m38.490s

16 Diniz
1m38.576s

20 Gené
1m39.972s

21 Mazzacane
1m40.462s

October 8 2000
SUZUKA CIRCUIT INTERNATIONAL RACING COURSE, INO-CHO, SUZUKA-CITY
CIRCUIT LENGTH: 3.644miles / 5.864km

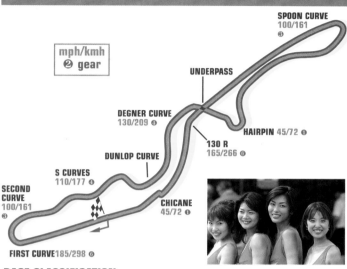

mph/kmh
② gear

SPOON CURVE
100/161 ❸

UNDERPASS

DEGNER CURVE
130/209 ❶

HAIRPIN 45/72 ❶

130 R
165/266 ❻

DUNLOP CURVE

S CURVES
110/177 ❹

SECOND CURVE
100/161 ❸

CHICANE
45/72 ❶

FIRST CURVE 185/298 ❻

RACE CLASSIFICATION

Pos	Driver	Nat	Car	Laps	Time
1	Michael Schumacher	D	Ferrari F1 2000-Ferrari V10	53	1h29m53.435s
2	Mika Hakkinen	FIN	McLaren MP4-15-Mercedes V10	53	+1.837s
3	David Coulthard	GB	McLaren MP4-15-Mercedes V10	53	+1m09.914s
4	Rubens Barrichello	BR	Ferrari F1 2000-Ferrari V10	53	+1m19.190s
5	Jenson Button	GB	Williams FW22-BMW V10	53	+1m25.694s
6	Jacques Villeneuve	CDN	BAR 002-Honda V10		+1 lap
7	Johnny Herbert	GB	Jaguar R1-Cosworth V10		+1 lap
8	Eddie Irvine	GB	Jaguar R1-Cosworth V10		+1 lap
9	Ricardo Zonta	BR	BAR 002-Honda V10		+1 lap
10	Mika Salo	FIN	Sauber C19-Petronas V10		+1 lap
11	Pedro Diniz	BR	Sauber C19-Petronas V10		+1 lap
12	Pedro de la Rosa	E	Arrows A21-Supertec V10		+1 lap
13	Jarno Trulli	I	Jordan EJ10-Mugen V10		+1 lap
14	Giancarlo Fisichella	I	Benetton B200-Playlife V10		+1 lap
15	Gaston Mazzacane	RA	Minardi M02-Fondmetal V10		+2 laps

Retirements	Nat	Car	Laps	Reason
Marc Gené	E	Minardi M02-Fondmetal V10	46	engine
Ralf Schumacher	D	Williams FW22-BMW V10	41	spin
Nick Heidfeld	D	Prost AP03-Peugeot V10	41	rear suspension
Alexander Wurz	A	Benetton B200-Playlife V10	37	spin
Heinz-Harald Frentzen	D	Jordan EJ10-Mugen V10	29	hydraulic pump
Jean Alesi	F	Prost AP03-Peugeot V10	19	engine/spin
Jos Verstappen	NL	Arrows A21-Supertec V10	9	gearbox

FASTEST LAP M Hakkinen 1m39.189s lap 26 (132.246mph/212.830kmh)

DRIVERS' CHAMPIONSHIP

1	Michael Schumacher	98
2	Mika Hakkinen	86
3	David Coulthard	67
4	Rubens Barrichello	58
5	Ralf Schumacher	24
6	Giancarlo Fisichella	18
7	Jacques Villeneuve	15
8	Jenson Button	12
9	Heinz-Harald Frentzen	11
10	Mika Salo	6
	Jarno Trulli	6
12	Jos Verstappen	5
13	Eddie Irvine	3
	Ricardo Zonta	3
15	Pedro de la Rosa	2
	Alexander Wurz	2

CONSTRUCTORS' CHAMPIONSHIP

1	Ferrari	156
2	McLaren-Mercedes	143
3	Williams-BMW	36
4	Benetton-Playlife	20
5	BAR-Honda	18
6	Jordan-Mugen	17
7	Arrows-Supertec	7
8	Sauber-Petronas	6
9	Jaguar	3

PETRONAS MALAYSIAN GRAND PRIX

THE BLOKE WHO WON THE FIRST THREE RACES OF THE SEASON ALSO WON THE LAST FOUR. SCHUEY MIGHT HAVE HAD TO TRY A BIT HARDER, HOWEVER, IF THE McLAREN DUO HAD BEEN WATCHING A] THE START LIGHTS AND B] WHERE THEY WERE GOING

Plenty of vroom at the Finn: Hakkinen leads DC and Schuey [main shot] into the first turn, but he'd had to jump the start to do it. As the Buzzcocks once sang [above], "Everybody's happy nowadays"

NO MATTER HOW HARD THEY TRIED TO BUILD THE EVENT UP, THERE WAS
something somnolent about the Malaysian Grand Prix. Ferrari
and McLaren made all the right noises about wanting to make
sure of/win the constructors' championship, but the highest thing
on most agendas was a much-needed holiday at the end of a
long slog.

In Sepang's heat and humidity, the majority of Formula One
personnel looked as though they would prefer to be dozing
under the palm trees. Mika Hakkinen certainly must have been
drifting off at the start because he took a leaf out of team-mate
David Coulthard's US GP book and set off before the race was
due to begin. He stopped again before the race kicked off, but
the damage was done and for the second time in three races one
of McLaren's drivers was assessed a jump-start penalty.

You couldn't accuse Michael Schumacher of napping, however,
because he took his fourth win on the trot – and his ninth of the
year. That equalled a seasonal record of which he was already
co-holder [Nigel Mansell won nine races in 1992, Schuey first did
it in 1995].

When the pressure is off, Schumacher rises above even his
customary best. He qualified half a second faster than his main
rival – and Hakkinen's faux pas simplified things further. It wasn't
all plain sailing, however, because Coulthard made his best
[legal] start for several races and beat the German into the first
corner from third on the grid.

Alerted to his own impending stop-go penalty, Hakkinen
dutifully let Coulthard pass – but the Scot compromised his early
advantage by running wide, bouncing across the grass and
filling his radiators full of dirt. With temperatures rising, DC
had no choice but to stop earlier than had been scheduled and
Schuey breezed into a lead that would be his for keeps.

With a clear track ahead Schumacher
launched a blistering attack and, by the time
he had made his first pit stop, on schedule,
he was still ahead of Coulthard. The Scot said:
"It was my own fault I had to come in so
soon. I goofed."

Before the start, Schumacher had
promised, if possible, to cede victory to team-
mate Rubens Barrichello, to repay the Brazilian
for playing a subservient role in Canada earlier in the season.

Coulthard put an end to any such gift-wrapped gestures,
however, by sticking around between the Ferraris and putting
Schuey under pressure in the closing stages. The flu-ridden
Barrichello was consequently miles behind at the end, although
in the circumstances he felt it had been his strongest race of the
year apart from Hockenheim.

Schumacher said: "It was a tight race and Coulthard really
pushed hard until the last lap. It was very tough. We were flat out
all the way. But he needed to go much faster to have a chance of
overtaking and there wasn't much difference between us in speed."

Hakkinen recovered from his 10-second stop-go – which cost
more than half a minute, by the time he'd driven in and out of

> # THE MAJORITY OF FORMULA ONE PERSONNEL LOOKED AS THOUGH THEY WOULD PREFER TO BE DOZING UNDER THE PALM TREES

**Fastest clap: Villeneuve
is welcomed by his crew
as he crosses the line
[above] fifth to bring
BAR's seasonal points
tally to 20. Below, de la
Rosa [far right] takes
flight after a pile-up for
which Diniz was blamed.
Funny, that**

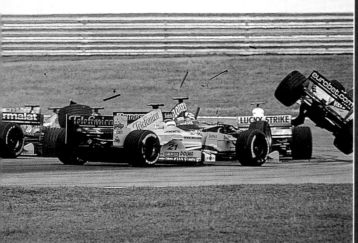

GONE, JOHNNY, GONE

If ever a driver deserved a break, it was Johnny Herbert [above, dicing with Mika Salo]. He got one during the Malaysian GP – his Formula One swansong – but it was not particularly pleasant, nor what the cheerful Englishman deserved.

Towards the end of a strong race [by the standard of what had gone before in a difficult season], the rear suspension of Herbert's Jaguar gave way and sent him hurtling into the barriers and out of the contest. Earlier in the afternoon, he had run as high as fourth.

Suffering a painfully bruised left knee, he clambered gingerly from his seat and was picked up and carried away by marshals. There was a certain irony in this.

When he made his F1 debut for Benetton in Brazil, 1989, he was still recovering from serious leg injuries sustained in a Formula 3000 crash the previous summer. On that occasion, he had to be carried to his car [although it didn't stop him finishing fourth, little more than 10 seconds behind winner Nigel Mansell].

Herbert said: "Given how I started my F1 career, I guess this was pretty inevitable. There's nothing like ending your career with a bang.

"I'm pretty disappointed to have a good race ruined by a failure such as that. When the car pitched, I was trying to work out which way I was going to hit the barrier so I could position my legs for the impact, but I lost my sense of direction."

At least Herbert had one claim to fame. His victory for Stewart at the Nürburgring in 1999 meant that, at the time of his departure, he was the last driver to have won an F1 race in anything other than a Ferrari or a McLaren.

Wurz case scenario [top]: why was he so fast? Science is powerless to explain

"ALEX DROVE PARTICULARLY WELL IN THE FIRST PART OF THE RACE. I HARDLY RECOGNISED HIM"
BENETTON BOSS FLAVIO BRIATORE ON WURZ

the pits – to finish fourth, although it took him three laps to pass Marc Gené's tidily driven Minardi en route. But for his penalty, the Finn's one-stop strategy might have paid off handsomely.

Alexander Wurz was the surprise of qualifying. With a freshly signed McLaren test contract in his pocket, the axed Benetton racer lined up fifth and drove strongly in the early stages before fading to finish just outside the points. Team boss Flavio Briatore said: "Alex drove particularly well in the first part of the race. Up to that point I hardly recognised him. Then after the first pit stop he slowed down and I recognised him again..."

Jacques Villeneuve took fifth from Eddie Irvine, who gave Jaguar only its second points finish of the campaign. That was rather better fortune than team-mate Johnny Herbert enjoyed in his 161st – and last – grand prix [see sidebar].

If Herbert wanted guidance about what to do next, Alain Prost could probably have given the Englishman a few tips [probably something about not becoming a team owner]. Seven years after the Frenchman retired from driving as world champion, he left Malaysia holding the wooden spoon in the championship for constructors, 10 places behind Ferrari and one behind Minardi, which was similarly pointless but had achieved mildly better results throughout the year.

It was obviously the culling season for antagonism in Formula One. After Mika Hakkinen's outbreak of all-round good sportsmanship in Japan, most of the so-called hard men of motor sport were falling over themselves to be nice by the time they got to Sepang.

Having raced hard against Michael Schumacher in the seasonal finale [left], David Coulthard [above] went to congratulate the German on his title success [a couple of weeks late, frankly, DC] and apologised for having been so openly critical of the Ferrari star earlier on in the campaign. The Scot said: "I just wanted to end the season in the correct way, so I apologised and told him he is a very strong champion.

"We've had some differences, but sometimes maybe I was saying things too publicly and not talking to him face to face. The longer you've been in this business the lazier you become. You get too lazy to walk down the paddock."

If anyone has the right to use that as an excuse, it is Jacques Villeneuve. The Canadian has spent the last two years parked at the far end of the pit lane, well away from Ferrari.

He wasn't about to start sprinkling platitudes at the end of the year, however. Jacques said: "Michael's had problems with me and I've had them with him. It's nothing bad, it just happens if you don't find the right atmosphere. It's the same if you're at school. In a class of 30 kids, there are some you like and others you don't."

STARTING GRID

October 22 2000
SEPANG CIRCUIT, KUALA LUMPUR
CIRCUIT LENGTH: 3.444miles / 5.543km

3 M Schumacher
1m37.397s

1 Hakkinen
1m37.860s

2 Coulthard
1m37.889s

4 Barrichello
1m37.896s

12 Wurz
1m38.644s

22 Villeneuve
1m38.653s

7 Irvine
1m38.696s

9 R Schumacher
1m38.739s

6 Trulli
1m38.909s

5 Frentzen
1m38.988s

23 Zonta
1m39.158s

8 Herbert
1m39.331s

11 Fisichella
1m39.387s

18 de la Rosa
1m39.443s

19 Verstappen
1m39.489s

10 Button
1m39.563s

17 Salo
1m39.591s

14 Alesi
1m40.065s

15 Heidfeld
1m40.148s

16 Diniz
1m40.521s

20 Gené
1m40.662s

21 Mazzacane
1m42.078s

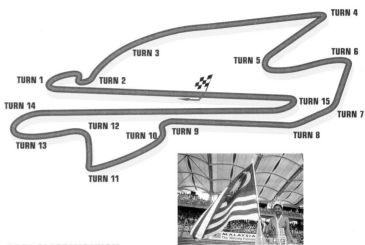

TURN 1, TURN 2, TURN 3, TURN 4, TURN 5, TURN 6, TURN 7, TURN 8, TURN 9, TURN 10, TURN 11, TURN 12, TURN 13, TURN 14, TURN 15

RACE CLASSIFICATION

Pos	Driver	Nat	Car	Laps	Time
1	Michael Schumacher	D	Ferrari F1 2000-Ferrari V10	56	1h35m54.235s
2	David Coulthard	GB	McLaren MP4-15-Mercedes V10	56	+0.732s
3	Rubens Barrichello	BR	Ferrari F1 2000-Ferrari V10	56	+18.444s
4	Mika Hakkinen	FIN	McLaren MP4-15-Mercedes V10	56	+35.269s
5	Jacques Villeneuve	CDN	BAR 002-Honda V10	56	+1m10.692s
6	Eddie Irvine	GB	Jaguar R1-Cosworth V10	56	+1m12.568s
7	Alexander Wurz	A	Benetton B200-Playlife V10	56	+1m29.314s
8	Mika Salo	FIN	Sauber C19-Petronas V10		+1 lap
9	Giancarlo Fisichella	I	Benetton B200-Playlife V10		+1 lap
10	Jos Verstappen	NL	Arrows A21-Supertec V10		+1 lap
11	Jean Alesi	F	Prost AP03-Peugeot V10		+1 lap
12	Jarno Trulli	I	Jordan EJ10-Mugen V10		+1 lap
13	Gaston Mazzacane	RA	Minardi M02-Fondmetal V10		+6 laps

Retirements	Nat	Car	Laps	Reason
Johnny Herbert	GB	Jaguar R1-Cosworth V10	48	rear suspension/accident
Ricardo Zonta	BR	BAR 002-Honda V10	46	engine
Ralf Schumacher	D	Williams FW22-BMW V10	43	oil pressure/ engine
Marc Gené	E	Minardi M02-Fondmetal V10	36	left rear wheel
Jenson Button	GB	Williams FW22-BMW V10	18	engine
Heinz-Harald Frentzen	D	Jordan EJ10-Mugen V10	7	hydraulics
Pedro de la Rosa	E	Arrows A21-Supertec V10	0	accident
Nick Heidfeld	D	Prost AP03-Peugeot V10	0	accident
Pedro Diniz	BR	Sauber C19-Petronas V10	0	accident

FASTEST LAP M Hakkinen 1m38.543s lap 34 (125.827mph/202.498kmh)

DRIVERS' CHAMPIONSHIP

1	Michael Schumacher	108
2	Mika Hakkinen	89
3	David Coulthard	73
4	Rubens Barrichello	62
5	Ralf Schumacher	24
6	Giancarlo Fisichella	18
7	Jacques Villeneuve	17
8	Jenson Button	12
9	Heinz-Harald Frentzen	11
10	Mika Salo	6
	Jarno Trulli	6
12	Jos Verstappen	5
13	Eddie Irvine	4
14	Ricardo Zonta	3
15	Pedro de la Rosa	2
	Alexander Wurz	2

CONSTRUCTORS' CHAMPIONSHIP

1	Ferrari	170
2	McLaren-Mercedes	152
3	Williams-BMW	36
4	Benetton-Playlife	20
	BAR-Honda	20
6	Jordan-Mugen	17
7	Arrows-Supertec	7
8	Sauber-Petronas	6
9	Jaguar	4

THAT WAS THE YEAR THAT WAS

THERE ARE 11 TEAMS IN THE WORLD CHAMPIONSHIP. McLAREN AND FERRARI SCORED 322 POINTS THIS SEASON; THE OTHER NINE MANAGED 110 BETWEEN THEM. HERE ARE A FEW THOUGHTS THAT OCCURRED DURING A TWO-HORSE RACE

Come on you reds: Schuey [top] won nine races – so his title seems fair enough to us. Inset, lots of Italians clamour to embrace a hot, sticky German. Above, a rare shot of the McLaren team without Mrs Hakkinen in the background somewhere

MICHAEL SCHUMACHER IS A FITTING WORLD CHAMPION. THERE, IT DIDN'T hurt too much to write that, did it?

The German might have his critics, but even they can't dispute his right to the title. He did, after all, win nine of the year 2000's 17 grands prix – and that is the name of the game, after all. Mika Hakkinen, more often than not his equal in terms of pace, won only four.

The pity is that a driver with such great gifts – and such a delicate touch, too, when it's needed – occasionally resorts to tactics unworthy of someone who has won more F1 GPs than anyone bar Alain Prost. By this time next year, he might well have hurdled that historic landmark, too.

It wasn't so much the Ferrari star's questionable startline weaving that grated [although other drivers persistently bleating about it certainly did], it was more the brusqueness of his manners at the best part of 200mph. His efforts to repel Hakkinen at Spa and David Coulthard in Barcelona spring particularly to mind. Ultimately, they will be recorded as close calls, no more.

Perhaps we were just lucky. Or maybe Schuey's judgement is so finely tuned that those looking in from the outside really can't appreciate it. Either way, the sport needs to get a handle on what is acceptable and what is not. It received a nasty jolt at Monza, in

TOP 10 DRIVERS

[1999 ratings in brackets]

1 [1] MICHAEL SCHUMACHER [left] Nine wins. Great race-craft. A bit too pleased with himself sometimes, but not without reason

2 [2] MIKA HAKKINEN Mid-season slump notwithstanding, he's a match for Schuey. There could be no higher compliment

3 [-] JENSON BUTTON Learns fast. Drives faster. Stunning. And he's only just about old enough to vote

4 [6] DAVID COULTHARD Occasionally inspiring in the face of adversity. But sometimes just off the pace. We don't know why. Not sure he does

5 [-] JACQUES VILLENEUVE [left]. Showed spirit beyond the call of duty. If they gave medals for fighting lost causes, he'd have a chest full

6 [7] RUBENS BARRICHELLO Fabulous drive at Hockenheim. But would he have won without that mad French bloke invading the track? No

7 [4] RALF SCHUMACHER Outstanding on his day, but much of the careful reputation nurturing of recent years was undone by Button

8 [-] MIKA SALO Dependable racer. Unfortunately, you could usually depend on the Sauber to be good enough only for about 15th on the grid

9 [-] JACK STRAW'S CHAUFFEUR Went faster on the M4 than Gaston Mazzacane went all season. And he didn't get a stop-go or even a token fine. Fantastic

10 [5] EDDIE IRVINE His Jaguar often looked like a 20-year-old XJ6 on worn shock absorbers. Eddie showed commendable spirit, all things considered

BEST CARS

1 FERRARI F1-2000

Italians [well, some Italians and a bunch of foreigners who live in Italy] build a car that works for eight months of the season, rather than just four

2 CITROËN XSARA PICASSO HDi Clever and spacious saloon. If you live in Germany, you can look forward to averaging 95mph and 40mpg on family outings

3 McLAREN MP4-15 Only won seven races? Rubbish by McLaren's recent standards

September, when a course worker died from injuries inflicted by flying debris – an unfortunate, freak accident that brought home the dangers that are sometimes blithely overlooked.

The difficulty for the FIA, motor sport's governing body, is that stamping down too hard on perceived over-aggression ultimately dilutes the sport and deters drivers from doing what many of them are paid millions to do, ie race.

There are those who argue that F1 has already become too sanitised – and tactical influences are such that what we are watching is effectively a 150mph chess match. In Ferrari technical director Ross Brawn, Schuey is privileged to have F1's equivalent of Kasparov or Karpov making the pit stop calls. Some of Brawn's rivals appear to struggle to tell the difference between a pawn and the queen.

Sharp wits have always been a fundamental F1 necessity. In Prost's Eighties heyday, tactics were no less vital, but it was down to the driver to balance tyre wear and fuel consumption to make the car as efficient as possible during a single driving stint that lasted about one hour and 45 minutes. Now, those things matter less. What you need is a bloke who can drive flat out in several bursts of 25-40 minutes while someone else worries about fuel strategy.

Unpalatable as it might be to purists – and Prost is among

4 WILLIAMS FW22
Former colossus teams up with slick new engine partner and remembers how to build decent single-seaters shock

5 MINARDI M02
The team's finest-ever chassis, no question. Effectiveness disguised by engine first used in Paris-Madrid road race of 1903

WORST CARS
1 Nick Heidfeld's Prost AP03
2 Jean Alesi's Prost AP03
3 The spare Prost AP03

MIKA HAKKINEN'S TOP 10 PRESS CONFERENCE PHRASES
1 The Michael
2 The David
3 The Rubens
4 You'd better ask the Michael
5 Maybe
6 I don't know
7 No
8 Absolutely
9 Yes
10 The Ralf

MOST DRUNKEN FANS

[1999 ratings in brackets]
1 [-] That French bloke who invaded the track at Hockenheim
2 [3] The Germans at Hockenheim
3 [5] The Germans at the Nürburgring
4 [1] The Germans in Austria
5 [2] The Finns in Hungary [above]
6 [4] The Germans in Belgium

F1 PERSONALITIES MOST OFTEN SEEN ON TV
1] Mrs Hakkinen
2] Gaston Mazzacane [being lapped]
3] Michael Schumacher

them, he'd like a return to the old system of start, race, stop, champagne – it is the unpredictability of pit stops that give modern F1 much of its spice.

The Japanese decider was a thriller, no question, but it might have been just as good – better, even – if the pit stops had been taken away. That would have compelled Schuey and Hakkinen to attempt a bit more in the way of direct wheel-to-wheel combat. Mind you, in those circumstances they'd probably have ended up in the gravel with bitter recriminations flying around.

Hakkinen, often a dour winner on the surface, reached hitherto unseen heights of eloquence after he knew he had lost any

SPORTS FANS LIKE THEIR HEROES HARD-EDGED IN THE HEAT OF BATTLE – AND MIKA HAKKINEN IS CERTAINLY THAT

chance of a third straight title – a feat unaccomplished since Juan Manuel Fangio did it in the Fifties. Along with his successful pass to deprive Schuey of the lead in Spa, this was one of the highlights of the year. Sports fans like their heroes hard-edged in the heat of battle – and Hakkinen is certainly that. But he was utterly gracious in defeat, a sharp contrast to some of the histrionics that accompanied his successful pitch for the title in 1999.

Early in the season, it appeared that Coulthard had gained the upper hand at McLaren with a string of performances that indicated he was the more likely of the team's two drivers to fight for the crown. Remarkably, he was mentally unscarred by the effects of a private plane crash before the Spanish GP. Two charter pilots perished in the incident; Coulthard, who handled the affair with compassion and dignity, was more badly shaken than he would admit, but still finished second in Barcelona only five days later. Because of the peculiar circumstances, this was the best performance of the year by any grand prix driver.

In the second half of the year, the Scot was less effective. Sometimes, as at Spa and Hockenheim, he was on the receiving

Ticket to slide, clockwise from top left: Hakkinen comes over all photogenic at Suzuka; Salo doesn't really merit a picture here, but this is nicely composed and it would be a pity to leave it out; Coulthard winning in France, before his mid-summer hibernation; Verstappen being spectacular but, arguably, ineffective

BEST PERFOMANCES

1] David Coulthard in Barcelona [left]
2] Steve Redgrave
3] Mika Hakkinen in Spa
4] Rubens Barrichello in Hockenheim
5] Michael Schumacher almost everywhere else
6] The Women's Institute against Tony Blair
7] Mike Atherton against the West Indies
8] Jean Alesi at Spa
9] Preston North End winning 1-0 at Fulham on October 24
10] Gaston Mazzacane for five minutes at Indianapolis

WETTEST FANS

1] Everyone at Silverstone
2] German campers at Hockenheim
3] German campers in Austria

COUNTRIES WE THINK HAVE TOO MANY GRANDS PRIX

[1999 ratings in brackets]
1] [1] Germany
2] [2] Germany
3] [1&2] Germany
4] [-] Britain

COUNTRIES WE THINK HAVE TOO FEW GRANDS PRIX

1] Italy
2] France

AWARDS

TANKER DRIVERS' ASSOCIATION MERIT BADGES FOR HAVING TROUBLE FINDING FUEL
David Coulthard in Hockenheim; David Coulthard at Spa

THE MANCHESTER UNITED EMBARRASSMENT OF RICHES TROPHY
To the German fans in Hungary. "Do we go to the campsite? The brothel? The bar? Or the licensed campsite/brothel/bar right by the circuit entrance?"

THE KEVIN KEEGAN COMMEMORATIVE SHIELD FOR TACTICAL NAIVETY
McLaren

THE ROY KEANE PRIZE FOR HIGHEST NUMBER OF EARLY BATHS
Heinz-Harald Frentzen, 11 DNFs in 17 races

THE VIDAL SASSOON AWARD FOR WEARING UNFUNNY RED WIGS
Ferrari – more Vidal Buffoon, frankly

THE TONY BLAIR/RIGHT GUARD TROPHY FOR LOOKING SWEATIEST ON THE PODIUM
Rubens Barrichello, Hockenheim

THE NOT THE MILLENNIUM DOME AWARD FOR BEING SOMETHING WE'D ALL PAY TO SEE
German F1 fans v William Hague. First to 14 pints

SPECIAL COMMENDATION TO THE ONLY MAN IN THE WORLD UNLUCKIER THAN JOHNNY HERBERT
John Prescott – he's got two Jaguars

THE WATER MARGIN PRIZE FOR AWFUL TV DUBBING
Michael Schumacher's L'Oréal shampoo ad. Not worth it, frankly

THE PHOTOCOPIER REPS ASSOCIATION AWARD [FREE LOAN FOR A YEAR OF A VAUXHALL VECTRA, PRESENTED FOR MOST OBSTINATE REFUSAL TO BE OVERTAKEN IN AN EVERYDAY 180MPH DRIVING SITUATION]
Michael Schumacher

FREE BSM LESSONS [IN A 1.0 CORSA, JUST TO BE ON THE SAFE SIDE]

To Pedro Diniz, for failing to notice other cars alongside him at 200mph [Schuey might be a vicious high-speed bruiser sometimes, but at least he knows what's where]

THE FREEDOM OF EQUATORIAL GUINEA
Awarded to the whole Prost team, for reminding the nation of Eric the Eel's tardy Olympic heroism every other Sunday

THE "WHY HAVE THE NEVILLE BROTHERS BEEN PICKED AGAIN?" PRIZE FOR UNFATHOMABLE SPORTING MYSTERIES
To TV directors everywhere. Why are the cameras always panning to Mrs bloody Hakkinen?

THE "WHY HAVE THE NEVILLE BROTHERS BEEN PICKED AGAIN?" PRIZE FOR FLAWED LOGIC
To ITV, for refusing to show the US GP live on terrestrial TV because Sunday evening schedules are sacrosanct. Only a few days earlier, however, they had shifted all the midweek soap nonsense to show Arsenal v globally famous Ukrainians Shakhtar Donetsk

THE NEWS AT TEN HYPE AWARD FOR COMMANDING TOO MUCH SPACE IN THE MEDIA
Nothing in F1, really, so we'll nominate all the tedious fuss about what time terrestrial TV stations choose to show their evening news bulletins. Does anyone truly care? No, in a word

Lost for words: the last caption in the book and I've got to find something interesting to say about Rubens Barrichello [top right]. Sorry, couldn't manage it

BARRICHELLO'S LONE WIN WAS REFRESHING, JUST BECAUSE HE'S A NICE BLOKE WHO HAS SPENT TOO MUCH OF HIS F1 CAREER IN SUB-STANDARD EQUIPMENT

end of peculiar McLaren pit calls. In Japan, however, he was simply outpaced by his team-mate to the tune of more than a minute during the race. Generally, however, he was as close to Hakkinen as he has traditionally been – and McLaren had no hesitation re-signing him for a sixth season. Hakkinen is regarded as one of the very best. Coulthard is seldom more than a tenth of a second or two per lap slower – and sometimes faster. Why would you want anyone else to do the job?

Barrichello's lone win at Hockenheim was refreshing, just because he's a nice bloke who has spent too much of his F1 career in sub-standard equipment. But the Brazilian is precious little nearer to knocking Schuey from his perch than the German's previous team-mate Eddie Irvine ever was.

As for the rest, Jenson Button exceeded expectations at the wheel of the new Williams-BMW – and the team's engine supplier deserves a pat on the back, too, for solid performances in its first F1 season since 1987. Benetton's integration with Renault can't some soon enough, because the team that gave Schumacher his first two titles was ineffective for most of the year.

British American Racing made solid progress in its first season with Honda and, thanks mainly to Jacques Villeneuve, was often a contender for best of the rest behind McLaren and Ferrari. Jordan, Honda's second team as from 2001, had a catastrophic year in terms of reliability – and wasn't helped when Benetton poached its technical director early in the campaign.

In its first F1 season, Ford's Jaguar-branded team fared worse than the Stewart operation [on which it is based] had done in 1999; Sauber continue to plod unspectacularly, but reliably; Arrows made a quantum leap forward to the upper midfield; Minardi had a good chassis, but antique engines; and Prost was so inept that Jean Alesi failed to score any points for the first time in a career spanning 12 seasons and 184 races.

Useless is too kind a word.